Sunshine + altitude + snowmelt + smart farmers = Colorado wine

It is not being flippant to address the query "Why Colorado?" in regards to winemaking with the response "Why not?"

It's certainly true that winemaking in other countries and other regions has a long and glorious history, but history and glory are limited only by vision and determination.

Those very qualities that make Colorado a marketer's dream — its diversity of landscapes and environments — are also what make it a difficult state in which to make wine.

Far from the temperate climate of northern California and the Northwest — cozily moderated by the nearby Pacific Ocean and elevations rarely exceeding 3,000 feet and in most cases barely one-third that — the last four decades have been a continuum of learning for Colorado winemakers.

Coloradans, though, are renowned for their determination to succeed in the face of odds, although in this venture it takes something more than brute strength to succeed.

The basic ingredients are plentiful.

1

There are cascades of crystal water tumbling too pure to purify from mountain peaks, sun-drenched days and cool nights to counter the short weeks of growing, and a community of farmers knowledgeable in bringing a crop to its peak.

What is it about high-altitude winemaking? Simply put, higher elevation vineyards have lower year-round temperatures, higher UV radiation (which leads to higher rates of photosynthesis), greater diurnal (day/night) temperature swings, and less oxygen and carbon dioxide.

There's also a shorter growing season, a key factor when deciding which grapes to plant.

But in the true pioneer spirit, there's an attitude of indomitability when it comes time to stick vines in the ground.

Not unlike earlier pioneers finding strength in community, early winemakers found that sharing ideas and techniques made a better future for them all.

Parker Carlson, his Carlson Vineyards one of the vanguards of winemaking in the Grand Valley, says his adventures in fermentation turned into a career when his home winemaking proved to be a "hobby that got out of control."

"Mary (his wife) and I moved over here in 1977 while I was working for Coors (Brewing Company)," Parker recalls. They purchased a tiny home on East Orchard Mesa because "we thought it would be a good place because we could get fruit" for making wine.

A few years later, when Jim and Ann Seewald moved their Colorado Mountain Vineyards from Golden, the Carlsons found the Seewalds an invaluable resource.

"They were very, very open" in sharing their winemaking knowledge, Parker says. "In 1988, when we finally started making our wine, there were Plum Creek, Colorado Mountain Vineyards and Pikes Peak. We were the fourth at the time."

"And I remember when we started, people started coming to us out of the woodwork,

Parker Carlson of Carlson Vineyards near Palisade

asking for advice," he says.

If you visit a winery and sit long enough, you still will see people coming for advice.

Yvon Gros, of Leroux Creek Inn and Vineyards in the lush North Fork Valley, is grateful for that early support.

"I knew going in that I didn't know anything about it and so I was counting on Horst (Caspari, state viticulturist) and those other" established winemakers. "I already knew to pay attention to the soil and what it needs and for the rest, I learned."

And what did he learn?

"I learned to relax. And I learned it's not written in stone, that you have to be a little flexible, that something different is going to be thrown at you every year.

"I also learned to sleep. That is one thing I didn't learn for the first three or four years."

That ability to adapt, being mindful of the lessons offered by the vines, is what Brent Helleckson of Stone Cottage Cellars in Paonia meant when he said: "In the last 20 years a lot of us have reliably figured out how to get a grape crop that looks kind of the same every year. And now, as winemakers, we've had 10 years of fairly consistent grapes, something you can work with to then understand how to make wine out of it."

Whether it is tradition, economics or simply someone's personal likes, what winds up most often in Colorado vineyards are the familiar European varietals found across the world.

But while the many microclimates across

Western Colorado foster some of the finest Cabernet Sauvignon, Syrah, Cabernet Franc and other vinifera anywhere, the land best-suited for those varietals is limited.

"It's a matter of choosing the right grape and then in the winemaking," says Joan Mathewson of Terror Creek Winery. Joan was Colorado's first winemaker with an enology degree and plies her trade at 6,417 feet elevation, making hers the highest winery in the northern hemisphere.

"Our climate is different up here," she says, casting a knowing glance at the vineyards outside her window, cascading in malachite rows toward the valley of the North Fork of the Gunnison River. "We're right at the top of the mesa and everyone who visits tells us, "Winter starts at your gate.' "

Still, "Up here, I knew Pinot Noir would work because it takes a short growing season. It does quite well."

However, the swing of hard winters (most recently in 2009 and 2012) shows how sensitive some vinifera are to Colorado's seasonal fluctuation.

That ubiquity of vinifera slowly is changing, but very slowly.

Like many other Colorado winemakers, Joan encourages exploration into cold-hardy hybrid grape varietals but doubts she will use them because of her success with cool-weather clones of Pinot Noir along with Gewürztraminer, Gamay Noir and Chardonnay.

Most growers are reluctant to plant hybrids for fear of lack of a market, and winemakers are fearful of putting hybrids in the bottle for the same reason.

"Someone has to be the first to jump and do both cold-hardy hybrids and vinifera," urges state enologist Stephen Menke at the Orchard Mesa Research Station of Colorado State University.

Guy Drew of Guy Drew Vineyards in McElmo Canyon near Cortez is one of Colorado's advocates in hybrid winemaking, offering a Baco Noir dry red wine grown in the brick-red soils of Montezuma County.

"This is the future" of Colorado winemaking, Guy affirms.

Stephen maintained the destiny of Colorado wines also may well be tied to what he termed "the maturing of the American palate."

"Wine drinkers no longer are dependent on the European style of 'Tell us what to drink,' " he says. "Now, young people don't care so much about geology but 'Does it taste good?' and 'Does it go with my food?' "

A thoughtful winemaker such as Yvon, who also is a culinary school-trained chef and operator of an exclusive bed and breakfast, knows well the intimate ligatures among good food, good wine and good people.

"When people say 'terroir' you think it's just the soil they are talking about but it's not," he says, looking around at the wholeness of his locale. "It's the climate, it's the people, it's the horses and the dogs, all the things that make this place what it is."

It's also all the things that make Colorado and Colorado wine what it is.

Guy Drew
of Guy Drew Vineyards
near Cortez

Grand Valley Wineries

Mount Garfield dominates the east end of the Grand Valley

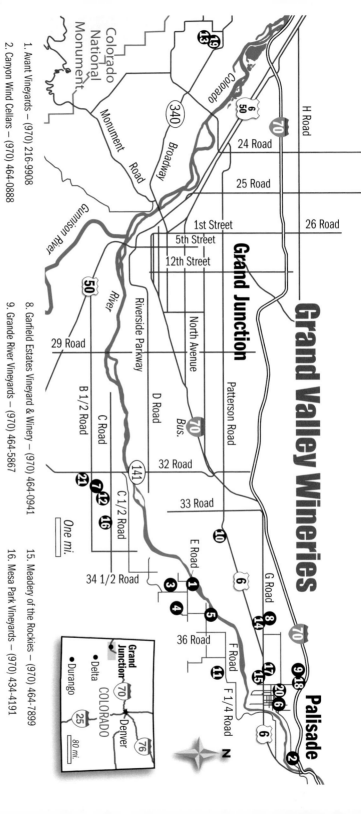

Grand Valley Wineries

1. Avant Vineyards — (970) 216-9908

2. Canyon Wind Cellars — (970) 464-0888

3. Carlson Vineyards — (970) 464-5554

4. Colorado Cellars — (970) 464-7921

5. COLTERRIS — (303) 956-6954

6. DeBeque Canyon Winery — (970) 464-0550

7. Desert Sun Vineyards & Winery— (970) 434-9851

8. Garfield Estates Vineyard & Winery — (970) 464-0941

9. Grande River Vineyards — (970) 464-5867

10. Graystone Winery — (970) 434-8610

11. Gubbini Winery — (970) 464-5608

12. Hermosa Vineyards — (970) 640-0940

13. Kahil Winery — (970) 640-3541

14. Maison la Belle Vie Winery — (970) 464-4959

15. Meadery of the Rockies — (970) 464-7899

16. Mesa Park Vineyards — (970) 434-4191

17. Plum Creek Winery — (970) 464-7586

18. Talon Winery & St. Kathryn Cellars — (970) 464-9288

19. Two Rivers Winery — (970) 255-1471

20. Varaison Vineyards & Winery — (970) 464-4928

21. Whitewater Hill Vineyards — (970) 434-6868

Colorado's wine industry epicenter

From one notably precarious outcrop where the ribbon-wide Palisade Rim Trail etches its signature across a cliff face on the east end of the Grand Valley, a watcher can inhale a view of the valley unfolding like a rippling canvas of greens and browns.

In the middle view, the Colorado River curls and bends in a westerly direction, like a snake shedding its skin, cutting a path between the farms, fields and vineyards blanketing the valley from south to north, east to west, near to far.

The byway encompasses Palisade and East Orchard Mesa

From this airy perch, a viewer sees how a silver thread of irrigation divides the green from the brown, followed by the realization that while the valley is large in scope, the cultivated area is smaller than first imagined.

In 1896, 14 years after the Grand River Ditch Co. (now the Grand Valley Irrigation Co.) was formed in 1882, a pamphlet titled *The Fruit Belt of Mesa County* related how the valley's climate and water supply were sufficient to support a bounty of "fertile fields and fruitful orchards" and that in addition to peaches, apples and cherries, several "European varieties of grapes" were being cultivated.

The same bulletin, however, cautioned investors that the "land that is adapted to the production of superior fruit is very limited," a verdict readily apparent 300 feet above the valley.

The comparatively narrow band of irrigated land is packed with growth, both human and otherwise, and among the battle over farmland it's the verdancy that catches one's eye.

The trailside promontory is a comfortable seat from which to view the valley and is made even more so by the near-constant breeze that cools and soothes on the hottest summer day.

The virtues of this breeze have been noted since the earliest settlers, but it was Norman Christianson, the enterprising original owner of Canyon Wind Cellars, who is said to have dubbed this year-round zephyr "The Million Dollar Breeze" for its temperature-moderating effect in the hottest summer and coldest winters.

Those are Canyon Wind's well-manicured vineyards you see laid out in careful grids along the Colorado River, and today they are under the watchful eye of Norman's son Jay Christianson and his wife, Jennifer, representing the first of Colorado's second-generation commercial winemakers.

That's a fine distinction, because wine has been made in the Grand Valley since the early 1880s, when European immigrants, among them

Italians brought in to work on the railroads and in the mines, planted their native grapes.

In 1899, Grand Junction founder George Crawford, recognizing the area's promise, planted what might have been the area's first commercial vineyard, a 60-acre tract of grapes and fruit along Rapid Creek above Palisade.

The Colorado wine industry was full of hope and promise and by 1899 the U.S. Department of Commerce was reporting 1,744 gallons of wine had been produced commercially.

Then, in 1916, temperance-driven Colorado legislators established a state prohibition four years before the national Prohibition went into effect, crushing barrels and dreams.

It wasn't until the late 1960s that the state's commercial wine industry reasserted itself, and by 1972 the modern-era of winemaking was under way with the planting of vineyards across the valley.

Today the Grand Valley has nearly 650 acres of wine grapes (85 percent of the state's production), boasts 21 (and counting) wineries and hosts the state's biggest, oldest and best-attended wine festival, the Colorado Mountain Winefest, held each September in Palisade.

In 1990, the same year the Colorado Wine Industry Development Act was adopted, the Grand Valley was designated a federal American Viticultural Area, the first of two such in Colorado.

An AVA designation recognizes

Grape harvest at the base of the Bookcliffs near Palisade

an area's special combination of soil, geography and climate.

In 2004 Carlson Vineyards' 2003 Riesling was named the best such wine in the world, and in 2010 Boulder Creek's 2008 VIP Reserve (using Grand Valley-grown grapes) took home Colorado's first prestigious Jefferson Cup as one of the top red wines in the country.

So much have the valley's wine fortunes grown that in 2012 a *Men's Journal* article extolled a bike trip along the Palisade Fruit and Wine Byway and Palisade was the ninth most-popular wine destination in the U.S., according to the travel website tripadvisor.

The Grand Valley has become the epicenter of the state's wine industry in spite of, or perhaps because of, more-populous cities elsewhere. Each year, the valley's aggregate of open space, climate, felicitous grape selection and amaranthine perseverance by pioneers and newcomers alike becomes more profound, like a wine steadily maturing into a harmonious blend of time and talent.

Avant Vineyards

3480 E Road, Palisade, CO 81526; (970) 216-9908; avantvineyards.com; avantvineyards@aol.com **Est.:** 2008 **Owners:** Neil and Diane Guard **Winemaker:** Diane Guard **Wines produced:** Sparkling, Viognier, Riesling, Rosé, Cabernet Franc blend, Sangiovese, Cabernet Sauvignon/Sangiovese blend and Tempranillo **Price range:** $8 to $30 **Annual production:** 300 cases **Tasting room**: By appointment. **Tours:** By appointment. **Other amenities:** Picnic grounds.

Winemaker's choice:
"Our 2009 Limited Edition Sangiovese paired with pasta with a hearty, fresh red sauce. Mmm! It's also sinfully good with chocolate!"

At Avant Vineyards, the principal winemaking philosophy is to keep the process as basic and natural as possible, letting the character of the fruit come through.

Wine is crafted in small batches from grapes grown on Avant's 9 acres of vineyards. Grown along the mighty Colorado River at the base of the 10,000-foot Grand Mesa are Cabernet Franc, Cabernet Sauvignon, Malbec, Petite Verdot, Riesling, Roussanne, Sangiovese, Sauvignon Blanc, Syrah, Tempranillo and Viognier.

Cool night breezes sweeping off the mountains meet the hot, sunny days of this high-mountain environment, helping the grapes acquire a tantalizing concentration of aromas, colors and flavors.

"There are amazing views overlooking the Colorado River and Mount Garfield. We also offer delicious, estate-grown fresh peaches in season."

"Don't leave our winery without first stopping to relax and enjoy our lovely view and delicious wines."

Canyon Wind Cellars: 'We grow everything'

I t was F. Scott Fitzgerald who wrote "There are no second acts in American lives."

So perhaps the rebirth of Canyon Wind Cellars isn't so much a second act but an entirely new play, where only the physical setting remains from an earlier time.

Founded in 1991 by geologist Norman Christianson, the winery and tasting room are set among a geometry of well-tended vines nestling in a crook of the Colorado River where it exits DeBeque Canyon and turns west into the Grand Valley.

Norman retired a few years ago, and today the earnest faces are those of Jay and Jennifer Christianson, Norman's son and daughter-in-law, who are continuing the development of Canyon Wind Cellars while focusing much of their energy on Anemoi, their own line of premium wines.

It's a dual immersion they embrace eagerly.

Jay and Jennifer, both in their 30s, are the first of Colorado's next-gen era of winemakers, connected by age and world-view to a generation of byte-savvy young wine lovers that increasingly gathers its wine education through the familial comfort of blogs, Twitter, Facebook and other social media.

They have their feet in both worlds, continuing the winery's tradition and reputation honed by its founders as well as developing new traditions from the prequel.

Despite the fast-paced change in social outreach, one timeless factor still remains: The two young winemakers know the best way to sell wine is to make great wine.

At both Canyon Wind Cellars and

The Bookcliffs near Palisade

Anemoi, that means starting with great fruit, and "we grow everything," Jay says. "We're also taking a more thoughtful approach to making wine from the vineyard."

Canyon Wind Cellars, with the seasonal guidance of Napa wine consultant Robert Pepi harmonizing with the day-to-day engagement of Jay and Jennifer, produces 12 wines: three under the affordable 47-Ten brand (named for the vineyard's 4,710-foot elevation); and seven varietals and two reserve wines under the respected Canyon Wind Cellars label.

Additionally, there currently are four wines in the vibrant Anemoi line, which Jay and Jennifer consider a winery apart from the paterfamilia of Canyon Wind Cellars.

"We respect what my father did and the great success he had with his wines, which continues today," says Jay. "But that's his wines, and these are ours."

Still, don't think Jay and Jennifer are treading water with their Canyon Wind Cellars lineup.

Their early influence has received considerable attention, including an enthusiastic reception by Master of Wine and Master Sommelier Doug Frost, who suggested the limited-edition (125 cases) Canyon Wind Cellars 2007 IV was the first Colorado wine worthy of a $100 price point.

"He said, 'It's time for the industry to recognize quality,' " says Jay of the Bordeaux-style blend of Cabernet Sauvignon, Cabernet Franc, Petit Verdot and Merlot.

The name Anemoi refers to the Greek gods of wind and unaffectedly links the wines to the steady down-canyon breeze that Norman dubbed the "Million Dollar Breeze" for its tempering of unseasonal frosts and winter cold.

The Anemoi wines, three lush red-blends named Boreas (north wind), Notus (south wind) and Zephyrus (east wind), along with a late-harvest Pinot

Canyon Wind Cellars near Palisade

Grigio called Iapyx (the northwest wind), tailor the opportunity for Jay and Jennifer to exercise their mindful grape-to-glass approach, a pursuit evinced in the Boreas, a wine described by Jay as a true low-intervention "vin de terroir."

Jennifer's honed palate directs the Anemoi line and doing so offers her "the perfect opportunity to dive into creating a style of wines that I love," she says.

"We made these to see what the vineyard could do and we've been very pleasantly surprised at their reception," Jay says, standing in the cavern-like barrel room beneath the winery, amid rows of oak barrels holding several vintages of wine sleeping until their release. "Our goal is to make the best wine for the property."

It is a goal adapted from the philosophy of winemaker Robert Sinskey, who has among his 10 points of winemaking, "Fine wines have a sense of place" and "Know your vineyards."

He might have added, "And keep the wind at your back," although in this case it's best to have Canyon Wind and Anemoi on your table.

Canyon Wind Cellars

3907 N. River Road, Palisade, CO 81526;
(970) 464-0888; canyonwindcellars.com;
info@canyonwindcellars.com
Est.: 1996 **Owners:** Jay and Jennifer Christianson
Winemakers: Jay and Jennifer Christianson **Wines produced:** Cabernet Franc, Cabernet Sauvignon, Chardonnay, Merlot, Petit Verdot, 47-Ten White (blend), 47-Ten Red (blend), 47-Ten Rosé, Port and IV (blend)
Price range: $13 to $100 **Annual production:** 5,000 to 10,000 cases
Tasting room: Open daily year-round 10 a.m. to 5 p.m.
Tours: Saturday and Sunday at 11 a.m., 1 p.m. and 3 p.m. from Memorial Day to Labor Day. **Other amenities:** Gift shop and picnic grounds. Outdoor event space for up to 200 people.
Ask for wine club details

Winemaker's choice: "Our reserve and Colorado's first $100 bottle of wine, IV, is a blend of 50% Petit Verdot, 32% Cabernet Franc, 16% Cabernet Sauvignon and 2% Merlot. It pairs fabulously with braised short ribs."

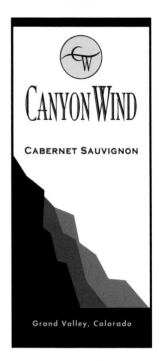

Jay and Jennifer Christianson are the state's first second-generation winery owners. The forward-thinking couple are putting their own stamp on Canyon Wind Cellars, founded by Jay's parents, Norman and Ellen Christianson, and named for the mountain breezes that fan the riverside 33-acre estate vineyard under the bright Colorado sun.

Renowned Napa winemaker Robert Pepi helped the Christiansons get started back in the early '90s, and he continues to be a resource and wealth of knowledge for Jay and Jennifer.

The couple produced the state's first $100 bottle of wine, IV. Over the years they've expanded Canyon Wind's offerings from only three wines to three distinct levels of wine.

Grown on site are Cabernet Franc, Cabernet Sauvignon, Chardonnay, Malbec, Merlot, Petit Verdot, Pinot Gris, Sauvignon Blanc and Syrah grapes.

The foundation of Canyon Wind is a river bench filled with loose cobblestones, sand and mineral-rich soils. Perched at 4,710 feet above sea level, the vineyard enjoys a high-altitude growing location without a significantly cooler climate or drastically reduced growing season that often comes with higher-elevation vineyards.

Canyon Wind wines have won awards, including a Jefferson Cup (Petit Verdot) and numerous Double Golds (IV, 47-Ten Rosé and Cabernet Franc— twice!).

"We offer the finest customer experience from our sleek iPad tasting menu to customized private tours and tastings. Guests can also visit with Finley, our Fine Wine Canine and the resident Winery Dog!"

"Don't leave our winery without first enjoying a glass of wine under our shady mulberry tree with an incredible view of the Grand Mesa!"

Carlson Vineyards

461 35 Road, Palisade, CO 81526;
(970) 464-5554 or (888) 464-5554;
carlsonvineyards.com; cobw13@acsol.net
Est.: 1988 **Owners and winemakers:** Mary and
Parker Carlson **Wines produced:** Chardonnay,
Dry Gewürztraminer, Lemberger (Tyrannosaurus
Red), Shiraz, Merlot, Riesling, Semi-sweet
Gewürztraminer, Prairie Dog Blush, Sweet Baby
Red and Sweet Gewürztraminer; fruit wines:
Pearadactyl (pear/apple), Peach, Plum and
Cherry **Price range:** $12.99 to $13.49 **Annual
production:** 10,000 cases
Tasting room: Is in a 1930 fruit-packing shed and
open year-round, seven days a week, from 10 a.m.
to 5:45 p.m. Closed Thanksgiving, Christmas and
New Year's Day. **Tours:** Upon request. **Other amenities:** Small gift shop with merchandise
from local vendors. A shady backyard bordered with flowers is available for picnics.

Winemaker's choice: "Our Laughing Cat Sweet Baby Red is excellent with barbecue ribs
and chicken. It also makes a great Sangria."

CARLSON VINEYARDS
LAUGHING CAT

2012 Grand Valley

Sweet Baby Red

100% COLORADO GROWN

Parker and Mary Carlson take the art of winemaking seriously — but they sure like to
have fun while they do it. Witness the cheeky wine names inspired by regional references:
Tyrannosaurus Red and Prairie Dog Blush. There's also homage to the Carlsons' love of
cats: Fat Cat, Laughing Cat and Cougar Run.

What started out as a hobby that overran their kitchen led to planting their own vines
in 1981. On 3 gravelly, sloped acres, they grow Riesling,
Lemberger (T-Red) and Petit Syrah. They buy Colorado-
grown grapes and fruit as much as possible for the rest
of their needs.

Parker became an icon with his red suspenders,
affable disposition and ready wit.

Carlson Vineyards' Tyrannosaurus Red was featured at
the Chicago Field Museum unveiling ceremonies of "Sue,"
the world's largest and most complete *Tyrannosaurus rex*
skeleton.

Awards of note include:
• World Cup Riesling Award at the 2004 International
Eastern Wine Competition.
• Best of Fest 2006 and 2007 for Gewürztraminer
at Colorado Mountain Winefest (only winery to win top
award two years in a row for the same varietal).
• Governor's 2011 Celebration of Premier Colorado
Wines for Best White Wine, Gewürztraminer.

*"Why make drinking
wine complicated?
Our idea was to
craft fine wines
that people enjoyed
drinking that were
affordable, friendly
and unpretentious. Our
belief is that wine is a
great accompaniment
to life — best with food
and friends."*

**"Don't leave our winery without first trying our Cherry wine with
Enstrom's semi-sweet chocolate on the rim of the glass."**

Colorado Cellars

The Vineland Corp. dba Colorado Cellars Winery, Colorado Mountain Vineyards and Rocky Mountain Vineyards; 3553 E Road, Palisade, CO 81526; (970) 464-7921 or (800) 848-2812; coloradocellars.com; info@coloradocellars.com

Est.: Colorado Mountain Vineyards in 1978, Colorado Cellars Winery in 1986 and Rocky Mountain Vineyards in 1990

Owners: Richard and Padte Turley

Winemaker: Padte Turley **Wines produced:** Alpenrose, White Riesling, Chardonnay, Gewürztraminer, Eclipse Sweet Red, Merlot, Syrah, Pinot Grigio, Alpenglo Reserve Riesling, Colorado Mountain Vineyards blend, Cabernet Sauvignon, Port Wine, Champagne, Roadkill Red, Golden Nektar Mead, Spiced Nektar Mead; 10 fruit wines: Cherry, Peach, Plum, Chokecherry, Raspberry, Blackberry, Pomegranate, Blueberry, Elderberry and Huckleberry

Price range: $13 to $30 **Annual production:** 20,000 cases

Tasting room: Open year-round 9/10 a.m. to 4/5 p.m. Monday through Saturday/Sunday.

Tours: Only on days not in production. **Other amenities:** Gift shop, picnic foods such as cheese-and-cracker plates, wine-based food items and picnic grounds. Half-acre lawn with gazebo that can accommodate up to 200.

Ask for wine club details

Winemaker's choice: "Trinity — Colorado's only Champagne — made by the traditional method of fermenting in the bottle (methode champenoise). Pair it with oysters and appetizers or enjoy with fruits or seafood or just by itself!"

Colorado Cellars pioneered the production of all categories of wine made in Colorado, with a history extending back to the mid-'70s.

Here is Colorado's oldest commercial vineyard, with vines planted in 1975 as part of Colorado State University's experimental Four Corners project. Now there are more than 12 thriving acres of Syrah, Pinot Noir, Merlot, Cabernet Sauvignon and Gewürztraminer.

Western Colorado's hot days and cool nights permit the grapes to retain high acid levels, which are essential to a balanced, long-lived wine. The high-altitude intense sunshine ripens the grapes quickly and evenly.

Since 1978 Colorado Cellars has been awarded more than a thousand wine awards. It is the only winery to have ever won the People's Choice Best Winery Award, awarded in 2000 at Colorado Mountain Winefest.

"We are Colorado's original winery — the first winery to commercially produce wines made from Colorado grapes."

"Don't leave our winery without first trying all 26 of our current wine offerings. Ours is the only winery in Colorado where you can taste all the categories of wine produced in the state: Grape, Fruit, Honey, Port and Champagne."

COLTERRIS Wines & High Country Orchards: 'This is our passion'

At first sight and first taste, you appreciate the singular experience of COLTERRIS Wines.

The sleek tasting room on East Orchard Mesa greets you with an embrace of emerald-green vines and precise rows of peach trees parading toward the horizon. At harvest time each tree is laden with fruit, luminous globes bright as Japanese lanterns.

Those sun-sweet peaches, enticing enough for First Lady Michelle Obama to visit in 2009, testify why the wines of COLTERRIS do so well, both in the market and in the glass.

"During one of our trips to Tuscany, we heard an old saying that you plant wine grapes where peaches grow," says Scott High, co-owner with his wife, Theresa, of COLTERRIS Wines & High Country Orchards. "And I thought, 'I know where great peaches grow.'"

When the Highs bought the orchard in 1999, their original plan called for ripping out the peach trees and planting grapes to supply Colorado's wineries because, as Scott says, Colorado wineries were "making a lot of wines but weren't making enough to have an impact on the market."

"As a wholesaler, the big issue I saw was there wasn't enough quantity at a reasonable price."

Stepping into the breach, the Highs decided to produce an affordable, high-quality Bordeaux-style wine. Or, as Scott puts it, "Offer a really good wine ... compared to the price you paid."

As part of the COLTERRIS sine qua non, the Highs developed vineyards with the same interweave of Napa Valley plantings used for the Opus One red wine of Robert Mondavi and Baron Phillipe Rothschild, a sharing of the sentiment expressed by Mondavi in his book, *Harvests of Joy:* "Making good wine is skill. Fine wine is an art."

Colorado River below COLTERRIS on East Orchard Mesa

When a visit to Nicola Catena, the celebrated Argentinian winemaker famed for his world-class Malbec, included him describing the terroir of his vineyards — 4,800 foot elevation, 9 inches of rain each year, volcanic-based clay, sandy loam — a light burned bright.

Theresa High, co-owner of COLTERRIS Wines & High Country Orchards

"I thought, 'That's just what we have,'" says Scott.

"We thought Malbec, for sure," says Theresa, or maybe it was Scott, for these two are of like minds, even if different palates.

Their give-and-take conversation is upholstered with fluency and laced with frisson, resonating with their desire and ability to absorb lessons from other winemakers.

They saw their dream as not a winery as cornucopia but as a committed focus on select wines based on traditional, 100 percent Colorado-grown Bordeaux grapes. The goal is reflective of the Highs themselves: open, approachable, attractive and unpretentious.

Their oldest son, Matthew, devised the name COLTERRIS, a melding of "Colorado" and the Latin word "terris," which refers to the earth, the synthesis a name remindful of other great wine names — Petrus, Dominus and Opus One.

It's that terra — the land and its climes — that lends signature to COLTERRIS wines.

"The cool nights and hot summer days are what makes our peaches so sweet," says Theresa, who oversees the vineyards, tasting room and peach-centric High Country Orchards while Scott tends to his Denver-based wine importing and distribution business, Classic Wines. "And that also is reflected in our grapes."

She adds, "We recognize you only have one chance to make a first impression, not only on the outside of the package but what's inside the bottle."

Theresa's extensive marketing background played a key role when, devising a means to attract more visitors to the vines and wines south of the Colorado River, she developed the Palisade Fruit and Wine Byway.

This 25-mile agritourism loop welcomes bicyclists and motorists on its round of vineyards, wineries, orchards and farm markets.

"My thinking was, 'How do we bring people off the highway and pull this community together?' Now, it's not only working for the consumer but for the wine industry as well. People don't come here for one winery; they come here for the whole thing."

From a winemaker's outlook, the "whole thing" means controlling the process from grape to glass.

"Our difference is we can and do control the grapes from the time we plant it to when we pick it and what we blend with it," Theresa says. "The reason we got into this business is because this is our passion."

COLTERRIS

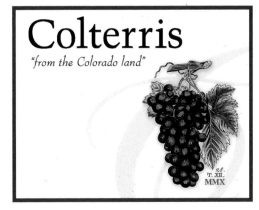

3548 E ½ Road,
Palisade, CO 81526;
(303) 956-6954; colterris.com;
theresa@colterris.com
Est.: 2010 **Owner:** Theresa High
Winemaker: Tyrel Lawson at Two
Rivers Winery **Wines produced:**
Cabernet Sauvignon, Cabernet
Franc and Cabernet Blanc **Price:**
$15 to $40 **Annual production:**
3,500 cases
Tasting room: 10 a.m. to 5 p.m.
daily from Memorial Day to Sept.
30. By appointment during the off season by calling (303) 956-6954. **Tours:** Three tours
daily at 11 a.m., 2 p.m. and 4 p.m. Memorial Day to Sept. 30. By appointment during the
off season. **Other amenities:** Country Store featuring fresh fruit grown on site, handcrafted
preserves, salsa and related products made from the orchards, vineyards, rose and
lavender gardens. Picnic grounds, light lunch and gourmet picnic items, fresh fruits, wine
products and local cheeses. Event facilities can accommodate up to 200 people.

Winemaker's choice: "Cabernet Sauvignon with prime tenderloin, lamb or other choice red
meats. Cabernet Franc with fresh cheeses, duck, poultry or salmon."

COLTERRIS Wines & High Country Orchards & Vineyards are family owned and
operated. Vinifera grape varietals of Cabernet Sauvignon, Cabernet Franc, Petite Verdot,
Merlot and Malbec are grown in vineyards on East Orchard Mesa south of Palisade.
Situated in the heart of the Grand Valley AVA, these 35 acres of vineyard land sit
at 4,800 feet in elevation, protected by the foothills of the Grand Mesa and by close
proximity to the Colorado River. The combination of high-altitude sunlight and cool river
nights produces distinctively bold red wines, rich in color, flavor and smooth tannins.
COLTERRIS Wines have won numerous Gold, Silver and Bronze medals and are
distributed throughout Colorado and other states.

*"At COLTERRIS we have a passion for making world-class wines
produced from grapes grown in Western Colorado."*

**"Don't leave our winery without first enjoying our aromatic
lavender gardens."**

DeBeque Canyon Winery

144 Kluge Ave. No. 3, Palisade, CO 81526;
(970) 464-0550; debequecanyonwinery.com;
debequecanyonwines@bresnan.net

Est.: 1997 **Owners:** Bennett and Davelyn
Price **Winemaker:** Bennett Price **Wines
produced:** Chardonnay (oaked and unoaked),
Gewürztraminer, Riesling, Viognier, Cabernet
Franc, Cabernet Sauvignon, Claret (Bordeaux-
style blend), Malbec, Merlot, Pinot Noir, Syrah,
Tempranillo and Fortified Wines (Merlot, Syrah,
Bordeaux-style blend) **Price range:** $12 to $35
Annual production: 3,000 cases

Tasting room: Three locations: DeBeque Canyon
Winery, Valley Fruit and Wine Shop at 757 Elberta
Ave. in Palisade and Coyote Creek Art Gallery at
419 Front St. in Fairplay, CO. The tasting room
hours at the Valley Fruit and Wine Shop are
9 a.m. to 6 p.m. summer through fall. The winery
and Coyote Creek tasting rooms are open year-round, seven days a week. Winery tasting
room hours are 10 a.m. to 6 p.m. May through September, and noon to 5 p.m. October
through April. Coyote Creek hours are 10 a.m. to 5 p.m. **Tours:** Offered daily if available at
the time requested and by appointment in advance. **Other amenities:** DeBeque Canyon
Winery and Coyote Creek tasting rooms feature art by Colorado artists. There are patios
with tables available for picnicking or simply relaxing at the winery at the Valley Fruit and
Wine Shop.
Ask for wine club details

Winemaker's choice: "Tempranillo, a Spanish varietal we planted
in the Grand Valley in 2000, has quickly become a favorite with
our customers. It is fruity and full-bodied with a spicy finish. It is
excellent with wild game, steak, spicy foods and barbecue."

*"We are a
family-owned
winery that
believes wine
is best paired
with food and to
be enjoyed with
family and
friends."*

Owner Bennett Price is sometimes referred to as "a pioneer of
the Colorado Wine Industry" for planting vineyards and helping
other wineries get started. He believes in long-term barrel aging to
produce smooth, full-bodied red wines and slightly dry white wines.

DeBeque Canyon Winery produces all its wines from grapes grown
in Western Colorado. Warm days, cool nights, higher elevation and
the minerals in Western Colorado soil create a grape that develops into fruity, full-bodied
wines. Price believes this to be especially true when conbined with allowing his award-
winning wines to develop through a good barrel aging process.

**"Don't leave our winery without first tasting all the wines.
We wholeheartedly believe that everyone's palate is unique
and that it's best when one understands that not all wines are
created equal. Try it ... you may like it!"**

Desert Sun Vineyards & Winery

3230 B ½ Road, Grand Junction, CO 81503; (970) 434-9851; desertsunvineyards.com; dkhovde@bresnan.net
Est.: 2008 **Owners:** Doug and Kathryn Hovde **Winemaker:** Doug Hovde **Wines produced:** Chardonnay, Cabernet Sauvignon and Zinfandel **Price:** $15 **Annual production:** 150 cases
Tasting room: Open 11 a.m. to 5 p.m. May to November, Friday, Saturday and Sunday. **Tours:** Upon request.

Winemaker's choice: "The 2008 Cabernet Sauvignon won a Gold Medal from Finger Lakes International Wine Competition and is great with any meat dish."

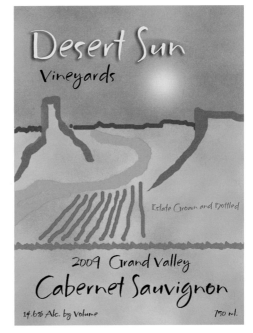

Desert Sun is one of the smallest vineyards and wineries in Colorado. But proof that great things often come in small packages, they've won medals with all of their wines, with the exception of the 2009 Zinfandel, which wasn't entered.

There is a 2-acre vineyard of Chardonnay and Cabernet Sauvignon grapes, with early-morning shade from the neighbor's giant cottonwood trees for the Chardonnay, and full sun for the Cab.

"We do this for the fun of it."

"Don't leave our winery without first asking directions to the closest winery!"

Garfield Estates Vineyard & Winery

3572 G Road, Palisade, CO 81526;
(970) 464-0941; garfieldestates.com;
info@garfieldestates.com
Est.: 2000 **Owners:** Jeff and Carol Carr
Winemaker: Rainer Thoma **Wines produced:**
Sauvignon Blanc, Syrah, Cabernet Franc, Rosé,
Viognier, Icewine and Chocolat Port **Price
range:** $15 to $20 **Annual production:** 2,500
cases
Tasting room: Open daily year-round 11 a.m.
to 5 p.m. except Thanksgiving, Christmas
and Easter. **Tours:** Daily upon request and
availability. For larger groups call ahead to
make arrangements. **Other amenities:** Gift
shop, and picnic grounds with great views.
Ask for wine club details

A converted 1910 barn at Garfield Estates houses the fermentation room, barrel cellars, lab, vineyard offices and tasting room. To Garfield Estates, the barn represents tradition and respect for the past. Jeff and Carol Carr like to uphold the traditions of winemaking, respecting the past and keeping things simple.

The term regional expression is something Garfield Estates is passionate about. The estate vineyard is focused on Rhône varietals: Syrah and Viognier. There are 17 acres of vineyards planted in Muscat, Syrah, Cabernet Franc, Viognier and Sauvignon Blanc.

The soils tend to produce a Sauvignon Blanc with more subtle stone-fruit mineral qualities, and the Cabernet Franc is a standout, producing a polished wine that many other regions might blend with other varietals. Western Colorado soils, however, manage to coax a great deal of complexity from this grape as exhibited in Garfield Estates' award-winning 100% Cabernet Franc.

"Our winery and estate vineyards are located on historic land homesteaded by the original owners 100-plus years ago."

Since 2002 Garfield Estates wines consistently have been award-winners both locally and nationally. Most recently the 2009 Estate Syrah won two Gold Medals in the 2012 Beverage Testing Institute World Value Wine Challenge.

"Don't leave our winery without first enjoying the spectacular views on our historic and picturesque property — perhaps while enjoying a picnic lunch, your favorite wine and some lively conversation."

Grande River Vineyards

787 N. Elberta Ave., Palisade CO 81526;
(970) 464-5867; granderiverwines.com;
info@granderiverwines.com
Est.: 1987 **Owners:** Stephen and Naomi Smith
Winemakers: Rainer Thoma and Stephen
Smith **Wines produced:** Sauvignon Blanc,
Viognier, Meritage White (blend), Chardonnay,
Syrah, Merlot, Cabernet Franc, Meritage Red
(blend), Cabernet Sauvignon, and sweet and
dessert wines **Price range:** $14 to $32 **Annual
production:** 5,000 cases
Tasting room: Open 9 a.m. to 5 p.m. year-
round, excluding major holidays. **Tours:** Offered
daily. **Other amenities:** Gift shop, picnic
grounds and event facilities for up to 500
people.
Ask for wine club details

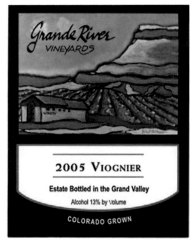

Winemaker's choice: "Meritage Red — our flagship wine — paired with any high-end cut of meat or a hearty pasta dish."

Grande River Vineyards was founded in 1987 when there were three wineries in Colorado — and they were chronically short of locally grown grapes. Founder Stephen Smith, impressed with the quality of Colorado-grown wines, decided someone needed to establish a commercially sized planting of grapes in Colorado.

In the early 1980s Stephen's career as an oil-industry landman had taken him to Denver and it was there, while taking wine-appreciation classes at the University of Denver, he tasted a 1985 Merlot from the late Jim Seewald of Colorado Mountain Vineyards.

It was a revelation of the potential of the Grand Valley.

Naomi became involved with the Colorado wine industry in 1994 and has been director of marketing and general manager since 1999. Her expansion of a popular summer concert series with nationally and internationally acclaimed musicians has taken Grande River into the 21st century.

Grande River is located at the gateway to Western Colorado wine country, near the Palisade exit off Interstate 70.

From its beginning as a grape-growing operation to supply others, the winery came to produce more than half the grapes in Colorado, making only 100% estate-bottled wines in traditional styles. The premium fruit is trucked to eight states for winemaking as far away as Minnesota, Connecticut and Texas.

"Join us for a summer concert on the lawn!"

Awards from more than 300 regional, national and international competitions for wines from all vintages to date attest to the quality of the grapes and wines.

"Don't leave our winery without first taking a walk through the demonstration vineyard to have an up-close and personal experience with nine different European wine varieties grown in Colorado."

Graystone Winery

3352 F Road, Clifton, CO 81520;
(970) 434-8610; graystonewine.com;
graystonewinery@aol.com
Est.: 2002 **Owners:** Barbara and Robert Maurer
Winemaker: Barbara Maurer **Wines produced:**
Red Port and White Lipizzan Port **Price:** $25
Annual production: 1,000 to 4,000 cases
Tasting room: Open daily year-round from
10 a.m. to 6 p.m. **Other amenities:** Gift shop
with wine glasses, wine-related gifts and fresh
fudge. Event space for up to 40 people.
Ask for wine club details

Winemaker's choice: "Our Port V that was
produced in 2005 has just been released. We
would pair it with Stilton cheese and chocolate."

Barbara and Robert Maurer grew up in
agriculture, being raised in the nearby Palisade
peach business. With Graystone, they've built a
boutique winery that is their family business.

The Maurers grow grapes on about 6 acres of
their 25-acre estate. The microclimate and soil
produce a remarkable vitality and character in
their grapes — Pinot Gris for their White Lipizzan
Port and Merlot for their Red Port.

They've won Gold and Double Gold awards on
all their releases.

*"Named for the gray,
majestic shale bluffs
surrounding the Grand
Valley and Colorado River,
Graystone is also close to
wild horse country. These
bluffs and mesas are still
home to a large band
of wild horses. It's truly
the wild, wild West and
awesome wine country!"*

**"Don't leave our winery without first asking about our French
bottles and hand waxing of our Port."**

Gubbini Winery

3697 F Road, Palisade, CO 81526; (970) 464-5608; gubbiniwinery@aol.com

Est.: Horse Mountain Vineyards in 1999, and the winery in 2011 **Owner and winemaker:** Linda Lee Gubbini **Wines produced:** Italian Amarone, Port, Malbec, Chardonnay, Pomegranate and Green Apple **Price range:** $14 to $20 **Annual production:** 150 to 300 cases

Tasting room: Open 11 a.m. to 5 p.m. April through October on weekends only. **Tours:** Available on request. **Other amenities:** Picnic grounds.

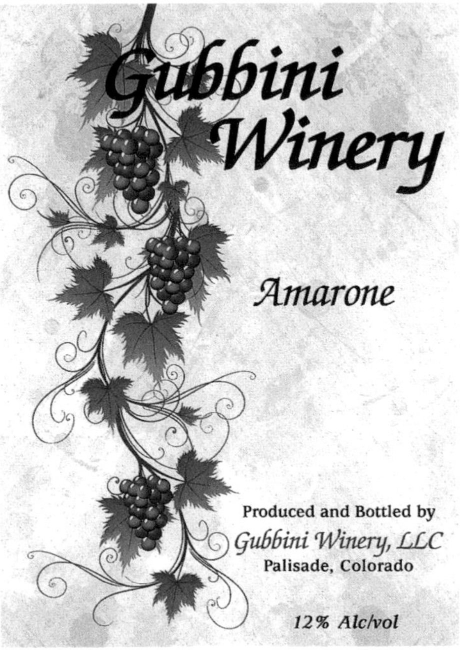

Winemaker's choice: "The Italian Amarone served with a meal centered around a pork dish of some sort."

Gubbini Winery

Amarone

Produced and Bottled by
Gubbini Winery, LLC
Palisade, Colorado

12% Alc/vol

After extensive research of grape varietals and consulting with Washington State University, Syrah and Riesling were selected by Gubbini Winery as the most compatible for the Palisade region and climate. The 3 acres of vineyards were recultivated in a former stone-fruit orchard that was part of an original East Orchard Mesa homestead.

After many seasons of learning the subtleties of grape cultivation, the yields improved and became recognized for their high quality. Presently Gubbini's grapes are being purchased and made into award-winning wines by prominent Front Range winemakers.

"Our homestyle tasting room features a bay window view of Mount Lincoln, a natural stone fireplace and a touch of hand-painted grape themes on the walls. Guests feel as though they just stopped by a friend's house for a glass of wine."

"Don't leave our winery without first taking a stroll through our beautiful vineyards."

Hermosa Vineyards

3269 C Road, Palisade, CO
81526; (970) 640-0940;
hermosavineyards.com;
hermosavineyards@aol.com
Est.: Vineyard in 1994 and
the winery in 2001 **Owner and
winemaker:** Kenn Dunn **Wines
produced:** Syrah, Cabernet Franc,
Cabernet Sauvignon, Merlot,
Chardonnay, Gewürztraminer,
Viognier, Rkatsiteli, Riesling and a
Rojo dessert wine
Price range: $15 to $50 **Annual
production:** 1,000 cases one year,
could be 12 cases the next
Tasting room: Open 11 a.m.
to 5 p.m. year-round. **Tours:**
Available when time allows. **Other
amenities:** Picnic grounds.
Ask for wine club details

Winemaker's choice: "Our
Cabernet Sauvignon pairs well with
cherry-wood smoked salmon."

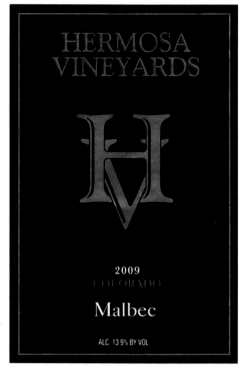

There are vineyards on site of the winery plus
a vineyard down the road for a total of 11 acres
producing 17 varieties of grapes for Hermosa
Vineyards.

Owner and winemaker Kenn Dunn describes the
Grand Valley American Viticultural Area as an oasis
in the high desert, with sunlight-drenched days,
cool nights and irrigation waters from the snow-
capped peaks of the upper Colorado River basin.

*"Hermosa Vineyards
is dedicated to hand-
crafting the finest
wine from grapes
grown in the high
mountain desert of
Western Colorado.
All of our wines are
produced in very
limited quantities."*

**"Don't leave our winery without first enjoying some great wine and
conversation."**

Kahil Winery

2087 Broadway, Grand Junction, CO 81507; (970) 640-3541; kahilwinery@hotmail.com
Est.: 2010 **Owners:** Tyrel and Kathryn Lawson **Winemaker:** Tyrel Lawson **Wines produced:** Malbec, Pinot Gris, Sparkling Muscat, Cabernet Sauvignon, Cabernet Franc and Malbec Blend
Price range: $15 to $24 **Annual Production:** 1,000 cases
Tasting room: At Two Rivers Winery, which is at the same location.

Winemaker's choice: "2011 Malbec, which has dark chocolate, black tea and earthy tones, paired with a favorite rib-eye steak or hand-cut prime rib. Also pairs well with a cocoa-crusted pork tenderloin."

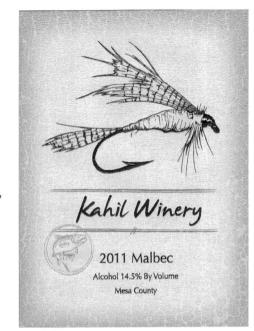

Kahil Winery
2011 Malbec
Alcohol 14.5% By Volume
Mesa County

Kahil Winery has 4 acres of Malbec and Pinot Gris vineyards in Eckert, which is an hour southeast of Grand Junction. Malbec grapes thrive in the high-desert climate of Western Colorado, which makes for concentrated flavors and colors and slightly higher alcohol.

Winemaker and co-owner Tyrel Lawson has worked in the wine industry for nine years. He worked up to winemaker for Two Rivers Winery while developing his own Kahil Winery.

Kahil has won Best of Fest/Best Red/Double Gold at Colorado Mountain Winefest, Gold and Silver at the Colorado Governor's Cup and Silver at the Beverage Testing Institute.

"We are one of just a few wineries doing Malbec."

"Don't leave our winery without first enjoying a taste of our up-and-coming wines."

Maison la Belle Vie

3575 G Road, Palisade, CO
81526; (970) 464-4959;
maisonlabellevie.com;
frenchy1972@gmail.com
Est.: 2004 **Owners:** John Barbier
and Gary Wright **Winemaker:** John
Barbier **Wines produced:** Merlot,
Cabernet Sauvignon, Syrah, Rosé,
Muscat, Petit Verdot and Vin de
Peche — a Muscat fortified with
peaches **Price range:** $18 to $31
Annual production: 1,200 cases
Tasting room: Open year-round
11 a.m. to 5 p.m. weekdays and
11 a.m. to 6 p.m. on weekends.
Tours: Offered occasionally. **Other
amenities:** Patio for picnicking or
enjoying a glass of wine. Picnic
food for sale, including cold-
cured meats, a large variety of
cheese, and savory and dessert
cheesecakes, French bread
and crackers. Amy's Courtyard
is an event facility that can
accommodate up to 150 people
for weddings, reunions, corporate retreats and private
parties, from casual to formal.
Ask for wine club details

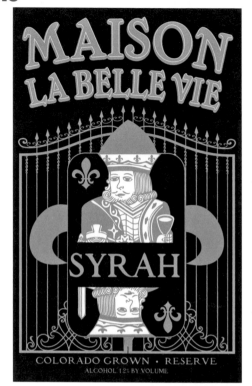

Winemaker's choice: "Enjoy the Merlot Reserve with a
steak and red wine sauce."

*"At Maison la Belle
Vie, French for 'House
of a Beautiful Life,'
we make European-
style wines that
are lower in alcohol
and meant to be
consumed with food."*

Maison la Belle Vie co-owner and winemaker John
Barbier grew up in the Loire Valley of France, where his
family has been making wine for 150 years. It proved an
easy transition from growing fruit in France to growing in
the high-desert region of Western Colorado.

Maison la Belle Vie uses the age-old method of dry
farming to achieve the maximum complexity of flavor in the grapes. There are 4.5 acres of
vineyards of Merlot, Cabernet, Muscat and Marechal Foch.

No pesticides are used on the vines, and very little sulfites in the wine.

Amy's Courtyard, named for John's daughter, is a popular and picturesque site for
weddings and other events.

**"Don't leave our winery without first ordering a glass of wine to
enjoy on the patio."**

Meadery of the Rockies

3701 G Road, Palisade, CO 81526;
(970) 464-7899; meaderyoftherockies.com;
glennf@talonwinebrands.com
Est.: 1995 **Owners:** Glenn and Natalie Foster
Winemaker: Brian Stevens **Wines produced:**
Traditional 100% meads: King Arthur, Lancelot,
Guinevere and Camelot; Melomel, or Fruit 'n
Honey wines: Apricots 'n Honey, Peaches 'n
Honey, Strawberries 'n Honey, Cherries 'n Honey,
Raspberries 'n Honey and Blackberries 'n Honey;
Dessert Meads: Blackberry Satin, Raspberry
Chocolate Satin, Chocolate Cherry Satin and Honey
Shere' **Price range:** $11.95 to $34.95 **Annual
production:** 5,000 cases
Tasting room: Open seven days a week 10
a.m. to 5 p.m. year-round. Closed for major holidays: New Year's Day, Easter, July Fourth,
Thanksgiving and Christmas. **Tours:** By appointment, during business hours. **Other
amenities:** A bee- and honey-themed gift shop with fun gifts, honeys, beeswax products,
garden decor and other novelties. Large gazebo with seating around the edges for
picnicking, and a welcoming front porch.
Ask for wine club details

Winemaker's choice: "Raspberry Chocolate Satin is a
delicious and decadent dessert mead made of raspberry
wine, honey wine and a chocolate infusion, and fortified up
to 18.5% alcohol. It is absolutely delicious after dinner and
would go superbly well with New York Cheesecake."

*"It is not surprising
that mead is at
the root of the
word honeymoon,
as couples would
traditionally drink
mead for a month
following their
marriage in hopes
of producing a baby
boy!"*

Meadery of the Rockery makes mead, or honey wine. Mead
can be traced back through ancient history in Europe, Africa
and Asia to approximately 7000 B.C.

There are no grapes in these wines. Instead, the meadery
uses Orange Blossom Honey and ferments it with water
to make 14 sweet libations in combination with a variety
of fruits and berries, such as cherries, peaches, apricots,
blackberries, strawberries and raspberries.

The half-acre of grapes on site are used for grape wines under other labels.

Owners Glenn and Natalie Foster have been deeply involved in the wine industry since
1976 and own two other wineries only a mile away: St. Kathryn Cellars and Talon Winery.

The meadery has won numerous awards and medals. Most recent was a Best in Class for
two wines at the Houston Livestock Show & Rodeo International Wine Competition.

**"Don't leave our meadery without first trying a few of our unique
meads and learning a bit about this ancient drink that is becoming
more and more popular every year."**

Mesa Park Vineyards

3321 C Road, Palisade, CO
81526; (970) 434-4191;
mesaparkvineyards.com;
bradwebb76@yahoo.com
Est.: 2004 **Owners:** Patty and Chuck
Price, and Brooke and Brad Webb
Winemaker: Brad Webb, Brooke
Webb and Chuck Price
Wines produced: Merlot, Cabernet
Franc, Cabernet Sauvignon, Barn Owl
Red, Barn Owl White, Riesling, Finz
dessert wine and dry Rosé of Merlot
Price range: $15 to $25 **Annual
production:** 1,000 to 2,000 cases
Tasting room: Open year-round from
11 a.m. to 5 p.m. on weekends and
Thursday through Monday from May
through October. **Tours:** Agritours
are available 1 p.m. Saturdays or by
appointment by calling
(970) 434-4191. **Other amenities:**
Picnic grounds.
Ask for wine club details

Young professionals Brad and
Brooke Webb in 2008 fled Denver
for a pastoral Labor Day weekend
of wine tasting in Western Colorado.
By the time they'd returned home,
they'd decided to buy a winery.

Brooke's parents, Chuck and Patty Price, joined as
partners and the two couples divided the labor of vineyard
management, running the tasting room, winemaking and the
business operations.

They agreed it was a big risk, but a welcome one.

There are 10 acres of vineyards at Mesa Park, producing
Merlot, Cabernet Franc and Cabernet Sauvignon. The vines
were planted from 1995 to 1998 and are irrigated from the
Colorado River.

Mesa Park focuses on hand-crafted, Bordeaux-style wines.

In 2012 the Barn Owl Red 2012 won a Gold Medal at the
Mesa County Fair.

"We are a small, family-owned winery and vineyard. We are growing grapes and making wine one bottle at a time."

"Don't leave our winery without first visiting our stony hillside Merlot vineyard to get a vantage point of our property and grab a fistful of our rocky soil."

Plum Creek Winery: 'Farming ... enhances an entire community'

Allusions to the narrative of Plum Creek Winery await you at the door of a well-appointed tasting room on the edge of Palisade.

A 7½-foot-tall chicken of sunburnt iron greets you with laconic whimsy; an equally aloof and weather-patinaed metal horse launches itself mid-gallop from a left hind foot; and three iron globes, linked one inside the other inside the other like matryoshka dolls, beckon the curious to push and spin.

The sculptures deservedly attract a bit of attention at this winery, one of the state's oldest, and observant visitors may discover those impassive statues offer more than visual relief. Ordained or not, they supply insight into the inclinations of Doug Phillips, the late founder of Plum Creek.

And like those self-encircling ferric globes, the stories of Doug Phillips, Plum Creek Winery and the Colorado wine industry are inextricably interwoven.

Doug, who passed away in 2008, lived many lives, from the hard-working son of a widowed chicken farmer in St. George, Utah, to that of a highly respected Denver attorney, to a pioneering winemaker, mentor and architect of the modern Colorado wine industry.

Doug is credited as the first winemaker to insist on using only Colorado-grown grapes, and in 1980, foreseeing a future demand, he and fellow home winemaker Erik Bruner planted vineyards on a mesa above Paonia.

By 1984 he and Erik had opened Plum Creek Cellars in Larkspur, and in 1989 the winery, with Erik as winemaker, moved to its present 5.5-acre site in Palisade.

In the coming years, as he and wife Sue Phillips directed the growth of Plum Creek Winery, Doug would mentor future winemakers; conduct key roles with the Colorado Mountain Winefest and the precursor of what's now the Colorado Association

Plum Creek Winery in Palisade

for Viticulture and Enology; and champion the Colorado Wine Industry Development Act, which oversees the state's wine commerce.

Today the winery's comfortable tasting room, with its welcoming couch and armchairs, hand-crafted barrel stave chairs, wine-related gifts and prominent displays of local and national artists, reflects Sue's initial vision of what was possible at a Colorado winery.

"Doug and Erik, being guys, thought tasting rooms should sell just wineglass and corkscrews and maybe T-shirts," says Sue with an incandescent laugh. "At first it was only (displaying) art from our personal collection. We thought it would make a delightful ambience and enhance the enjoyment of the wine."

Now it's an oft-repeated meme in tasting rooms around the state, a taking notice that wine-astute consumers seek more in a tasting room than simply a lineup of bottles and sparkling glasses.

Sharing that enjoyment of wine, specifically Colorado wine made from grapes grown no more than a bicycle ride away, was part of Plum Creek's overall muse.

"Our vision at the time was a desire to build something that was new to Colorado and have benefits extending beyond the things we were doing in our law practice," says Sue of their focus on worker's compensation. "We both were doing the kind of work where we help people, but with farming, it enhances an entire community.

"We couldn't foresee what it is today, but we knew we were building something new and

if you did it the right way, and if the wines are good, you are going to build excitement with people who otherwise have no connection with wine."

It's molding those connections, bringing people and ideas and passions together at the right time, something the Greek classicists call hora, which may have been Doug's greatest talent, even if he never realized it.

His gentle humor (the whimsical chicken, remember?), overarching commitment to Colorado wines and subtle intricacies spilled over to everyone he touched, and today there isn't a winery or winemaker in the state without some element of Doug Phillips' legacy.

The evidence of this legacy is just beyond the door, past the iron globes and resolute horse and droll chicken.

There, you see Palisade, an industrious farming community quite comfortable in its own skin and yet, thanks to the unfolding of a wine industry, emerging like a chrysalis from its cocoon.

"Palisade was a very different town in 1988 when Plum Creek moved here," ventures Sue. "What a difference the wineries have made in this little town."

7½-foot-tall chicken sculpture at Plum Creek Winery in Palisade

Plum Creek Winery

3708 G Road, Palisade, CO 81526; (970) 464-7586; plumcreekwinery.com; plumcreekwinery@att.net

Est.: 1984 **Owner:** Sue Phillips **Winemaker:** Jenne Baldwin-Eaton **Wines produced:** Chardonnay, Cabernet Sauvignon, Sauvignon Blanc, Cabernet Franc, Merlot, Riesling, Palisade Red, Palisade Rosé, Palisade Festival, Late Harvest Somerset, Late Harvest Sauvignon Blanc and Grand Mesa Reserve.

Price range: $10 to $32 **Annual production:** 12,000 to 13,000 cases

Tasting room: Open daily 10 a.m. to 5 p.m., except Thanksgiving, Christmas and New Year's Day. **Tours:** On request; by appointment for large groups. **Other amenities:** Picnic grounds. The gift shop features locally made artwork and unique, eclectic gifts.

COLORADO

PLUM ● CREEK

2006

GRAND MESA

COLORADO GROWN

Winemaker's choice: "Plum Creek's premium reserve red wine, Grand Mesa, with prosciutto and portabella mushroom lasagna. Grand Mesa offers ripe berry and deep cherry tones laced with leather and cedar. With a velvety structure, this supple wine is highlighted by two years' aging, with complex tones of French and American oak."

Plum Creek Winery specializes in award-winning wines made from locally sourced grapes grown only in Colorado. It has been continuously licensed since 1984.

The vineyards, totaling 48 acres, are located in Palisade and Paonia, two distinctive viticultural areas. Vineyards in both areas are planted in river valleys, which concentrates the effect of canyon breezes, moderating hot summer weather and insulating from cold temperatures in winter and spring.

Proximity to the Colorado River in Palisade and to the North Fork of the Gunnison in Paonia provides water for irrigation and helps raise humidity, which can ease the sometimes harsh heat of summer.

"Plum Creek has a friendly and knowledgeable tasting room staff, welcoming guests to feel at home while sampling Plum Creek's European-style wines in an elegant tasting room filled with antique furniture, Oriental rugs and fine art."

Plum Creek won its first Gold Medal in an international wine competition for its 1987 Merlot at the 1989 International Eastern Wine Competition. Plum Creek's wines have been awarded more than 400 medals including multiple Double Gold Medals, in international wine competitions, along with repeat awards as Wine of the Year by *The Denver Post* and the Colorado Mountain Winefest. In 2011 and 2012 Plum Creek's wines were awarded the Governor's Cup for Best Colorado White Wine and Best Colorado Dessert Wine.

In 2008, *Time* magazine selected Plum Creek's Grand Mesa as the sole Colorado wine in its article, "The United States of Wine." Also, Plum Creek's Redstone Reserve Chardonnay received a mention in Clive Cussler's international bestseller, *Shock Wave*.

"Don't leave our winery without first having your picture taken with the winery's mascot, Chardonnay Chicken, a 7½-foot-tall sculpture, or the running horse, Big Red, both by local artist Lyle Nichols."

Summit Cellars

595 36 Road, Palisade, CO
81526; (970) 361-4980;
SummitCellars@msn.com
Est.: 2001 **Owners:** Vaughn and
Lynn Goebel **Winemaker:** Vaughn
Goebel **Wines produced:** Cabernet,
Chardonnay, Merlot and Pinot Noir
Price range: $12 to $20 **Annual
production:** Small batches
No tasting room or tours. Wine
is available only at local retailers
including Andy's Liquor Mart,
Coronado Liquor Mart, East Valley
Liquors and Peachwood Liquor.

Summit Cellars

2011
Estate Bottled
Grand Valley
Pinot Noir

Produced and bottled by
Summit Cellars, Palisade, CO

12% Alc/vol   750ml

Winemaker's choice: "Peach Country Chardonnay; pair it with sliced Palisade peaches, fish or chicken."

Summit Cellars is a home-based avocation for winemaker Vaughn Goebel, but he has plans to expand and add a tasting room in the future.

There is some interesting history at Summit, which has some of the oldest vines in the valley on 5 acres planted in Cabernet Sauvignon, Chardonnay, Merlot and Pinot Noir. These older vines produce less fruit, but more intense flavors.

One way for the small upstart to garner attention has been by bottling some batches in Mason jars. Retailers either love it or hate it, finding it either charming or hokey.

All wines also are available in traditional bottles, at the retailer's choice.

Family owned and operated, Summit uses natural farming practices, working by hand from pruning, to picking, to the final wine in your glass.

"Don't leave our winery without first ... well, you can't really come to our winery yet. But look for a tasting room in the future!"

Talon Winery & St. Kathryn Cellars

785 Elberta Ave., Palisade, CO 81526;
(970) 464-9288; stkathryncellars.com;
glennf@talonwinebrands.com
Est.: 1999 **Owners:** Glenn and Natalie Foster
Winemaker: Brian Stevens **Wines produced:**
Chardonnay, Viognier, Riesling, Merlot, Cabernet
Sauvignon, Port, Gewürztraminer and Moscato,
plus several special blends **Price range:** $13.95
to $19.95 **Annual Production:** 6,000 cases,
between the two brands
Tasting room: Open 10 a.m. to 5 p.m. seven
days a week year-round. Closed for major
holidays: New Year's Day, Easter, July Fourth,
Thanksgiving and Christmas. **Tours:** Available
by appointment at sister winery, Meadery of the
Rockies. **Other amenities:** The gift shop offers
the largest selection of wine-related gifts in the
state. Very large lawn, suitable for picnic blankets,
or bring your own seating.
Ask for wine club details

Winemaker's choice: "Our Gewürztraminer
won a Gold Medal and was designated the best
Germanic Aromatic wine in Colorado at the Governor's Cup in 2013."

Talon Winery is dedicated to locally grown grape
wines such as Chardonnay, Viognier, Cabernet Sauvignon,
Riesling and Merlot. Wines made under the St. Kathryn
Cellars label include light-hearted and extremely popular
creations such as Lavender, Cranberry Kiss, Blueberry
Bliss and Peach Passion.

The family-owned business has been deeply involved in
the wine industry since 1976.

The Fosters believe their wines exhibit excellent
varietal character as well as distinguishing terroir. In their
reds, that translates to a dry mineral character. In their
whites, it is not as pronounced.

All grapes for the Talon label come from local growers.

Talon Winery won 21 awards at the Denver International Wine Competition in 2012 and
11 of those were Gold.

Talon won 26 awards at the Governor's Cup Wine Competition in 2013.

*"We own another
unique winery only a
mile away: Meadery
of the Rockies. If you
join our wine club you
can choose from any
of our 42 different
wines."*

**"Don't leave our winery without first trying our Lavender wine. It
sounds strange, but it is our number-one seller across all 42 wines."**

Two Rivers Winery: A French chateau 'out on the plains'

On any given day, the owner of Two Rivers Winery & Chateau is: overseeing his own winery while encouraging and mentoring other Colorado winemakers; serving in multiple roles on state and local wine boards; and opening doors for his singularly promising young winemaker.

Above all, Bob Witham is working to ensure wine drinkers never experience the reason he got into this business: by tasting a poorly made Colorado wine.

Bob's advocacy for Colorado winemaking began in 1999 with an economic false-start. Plans to build an upscale, seniors-only gated community were put aside when the demographics wouldn't work out.

In its stead rose a winery and stately chateau amidst rows of malachite grapevines at the toe of the mahogany-stained Wingate sandstone cliffs fronting Colorado National Monument.

Between the scrapped seniors' residences and the French country-design chateau came fate in a bottle.

"Someone had previously given us a bottle of Colorado wine and (when) we decided not to do the patio home project, Billie and I had it that night," recalls Bob, his measured tone portending bad news. "It wasn't very good."

Perplexed, Bob turned to his wife and said, "I wonder why it is that they grow these great peaches that the president can carry around on his airplane, but they seemingly can't grow good grapes to make good wines?"

That question, he recalls, "turned into a research project and (that) turned into this, so it was almost serendipitous."

Serendipity evolved into one of Colorado's largest wineries and perhaps the only winery with a wedding facility whose first customers didn't drink.

Before the chateau was built, "we were doing weddings at our pavilion," says Bob. "Our first wedding booked

Two Rivers Winery & Chateau in Grand Junction

was Mennonites. They came in buggies and they don't drink."

And the second and third weddings were Mennonites, also.

"Billie and I could see this wasn't going to work for a winery, so we started having a $500 minimum bar as part of the deal."

The chateau is elegant but, equally important, it's part of a business plan, something the MBA-educated Bob finds all-too lacking in other wineries.

"It's really a pretty simple concept," he offers. "If you're selling wine, you need to get brand recognition."

When he and Billie were planning the winery/chateau facility, brand recognition included offering visitors a place to savor wines other than the typical tasting room.

"Our objective wasn't to have a bed and breakfast," he says. "If we could create an environment where people could come and taste wine in a celebratory environment, that would be double whammy in a positive way for us."

"Out on the plains" is how Bob describes the winery's location as the western-most of the Grand Valley's wineries.

"We are just on the cusp of things," he says. "Napa Valley has one microclimate, per se, but here we have all kinds of microclimates. In Colorado it's raining on one side of the street and sun shining on the other."

The vines around the chateau offer more than eye relief. In 2013 the acreage was replanted with the cold-hardy hybrid varietals Baco Noir and La Crescent, a working test plot for Colorado's winemaking potential.

Unlike wineries offering two dozen or more wines, Bob is quite content with the eight wines bearing Two Rivers' name.

"I don't know what the magic number is," he says. "But for us, the business aspect of it is (you) don't get so many varieties you can't control those varieties."

His vision included pushing for the state's shared premise law, adopted in 2008. This law opened Two Rivers' winemaking facilities to winemaker Tyrel Lawson, where he creates both the Two Rivers and his own Kahil line of wines.

"My object was to create opportunities for Tyrel so I could keep him around as winemaker and get him involved more in the wine industry."

Now, he and Billie find more would-be winemakers are seeking their advice.

The Withams offer it gladly although sagely, seeing the wine industry as an extended family sometimes in need of direction.

"For us, it's the relationships you have with people."

The chateau is popular for weddings

Two Rivers Winery

2087 Broadway, Grand Junction, CO 81507; (970) 255-1471; tworiverswinery.com; bob@tworiverswinery.com

Est.: 1999 **Owners:** Bob and Billie Witham **Winemaker:** Tyrel Lawson **Wines produced:** Chardonnay, Merlot, Riesling, Cabernet Sauvignon, Port, Vintner's Blend and Rosé **Price range:** $12.75 to $16.75 **Annual production:** 14,000 cases

Tasting room: Open year-round 10:30 a.m. to 6 p.m. Monday through Saturday and noon to 5 p.m. Sunday **Tours:** Yes, if not extremely busy. For 10 or more people there is a $4 charge per person, but it is reduced

by that same amount if wine purchases achieve the charge. There's also a virtual tour of winemaking activities. **Other amenities:** Gift shop with all sorts of wine-related items. Also beautiful customized etched wine bottles (one case minimum). Picnic grounds. A full catering kitchen is available for special events. Country Inn and a Chateau Conference/ Event Center. Can accommodate 175 sit-down guests.

Ask for wine club details

Winemaker's choice: "People love our Riesling with Thanksgiving Dinner as well as Thai food."

Two Rivers Winery is an elegant destination winery with expansive amenities, and the view's not bad, either. The outdoor pavilion and grounds are surrounded by Colorado National Monument to the southwest, the Bookcliffs to the north and Grand Mesa to the east. Lodging is available at their Country Inn, and the Chateau Conference/Event Center is popular for weddings, reunions and corporate retreats.

On site are 15 acres of Chardonnay, Merlot and Cabernet Sauvignon grapes that exhibit what Two Rivers refers to as orchard flavors such as berries, cherries, pears and apples. Two Rivers wines are more akin to Old World wines.

Two Rivers has garnered 36 Gold Medals in international competitions.

"We do not pay lip service to quality. It is at the essence of what we do, and we believe that since quality can be measured, then we can always improve upon our products."

"Don't leave our winery without first spending some time with our people. Our average length of time our employees have been with us is 11.5 years. They are extremely knowledgeable and are willing to share what they know with our customers."

Varaison Vineyards & Winery

405 W. First St., Palisade, CO
81526; (970) 464-4928
varaisonvineyards.com;
info@varaisonvineyards.com
Est.: 2004 **Owners:** Ron and Kristin
West **Winemaker:** Ron West **Wines
produced:** Merlot, Chardonnay,
Barbera, Orange Moscato and Black
Moscato **Price range:** $12 to $45
Tasting room: Open 10 a.m. to
5 p.m. daily, year-round. **Tours:**
Daily upon request. **Other
amenities:** Events for up to 400 in
the David Austin Rose Garden, and
up to 250 in the open-air pavilion.
Conference room for up to 12.
Picnic grounds with full catering available.

Winemaker's choice: "Crème Brulee Chardonnay paired with ripe pear in Chardonnay reduction, butter and Madagascar Bourbon vanilla, with melted triple cream brie. OMG!"

Located in the heart of Palisade, Varaison Vineyards & Winery converted a 100-year-old Victorian mansion into a beautifully restored tasting room.

The winery has a sweeping veranda, and expansive gardens of roses, wildflowers and sweet French lavender.

Varaison has the largest mass planting of David Austin Old English Roses in North America. Styled after the internationally recognized Nyman's Garden in East Sussex, England, the garden establishes 1,400 roses in a formal walking garden.

A large gazebo in the garden center was moved from Denver. The massive beams and wood frame were selected from a historic hay barn originally built in 1897.

On site are 8.5 acres of Merlot, Chardonnay, Orange Moscato, Barbera and Nebbiolo.

"Varaison Vineyards & Winery is Colorado's premier Victorian destination venue."

"Don't leave our winery without first enjoying our Old English Rose gardens."

Whitewater Hill Vineyards

220 32 Road, Grand Junction, CO 81503;
(970) 434-6868; whitewaterhill.com;
info@whitewaterhill.com

Est.: Vineyard planted in 1998 and winery opened in 2004 **Owners:** Nancy Janes and John Behrs **Winemaker:** Nancy Janes
Wines produced: Sauvignon Blanc, "No Oak" Chardonnay, "Barrel Select" Chardonnay, Viognier, Shiraz, Merlot, Cabernet Franc, Cabernet Sauvignon, Ethereal, White Merlot, Gewürztraminer, Riesling, Muscat Canelli, Late Harvest Riesling, Sweetheart Red, Crag Crest Ruby Classico (Port style), Zero Below and Riesling Icewine **Price range:** $10 to $60
Annual production: 2,000 cases
Tasting room: Noon to 6 p.m. most days. Call ahead for hours in January and February.
Tours: Only by special request and depending on staff availability.
Other amenities: Picnic grounds and gift shop.
Ask for wine club details

Winemaker's choice: "Zero Below Late Harvest Chardonnay and Palisade peach pie."

Whitewater Hill Vineyards has 6.5 acres of vineyards at the winery overlooking the Colorado River creasing the Grand Valley floor below, and 24 acres of grapes overall. Whitewater Hill produces classic varietal wines and grows Cabernet Sauvignon, Cabernet Franc, Merlot, Shiraz, Muscat Canelli, Chardonnay and Riesling.

Grapes grown in this ancient seabed of mineral-rich limestone soils take on wonderful aromatic qualities from the high elevation and intense sunlight. Whitewater Hill makes wine with a clean, fruit-forward style. All wines are 100% Grand Valley grown.

One of only two wineries in the state to produce an icewine, Whitewater Hill leaves some grapes on the vine to ripen all through fall and be nipped by Jack Frost. When the super-ripe grapes are frozen in November or December, they are picked and pressed immediately into an intensely rich and sweet wine with tropical overtones.

What bribe can be made to entice a few brave and hearty friends to harvest in single-digit temperatures? A free bottle of icewine!

"Don't leave our winery without first trying our Whitewater Hill Icewine, which was picked as supersweet frozen berries in mid-December and has an alluring medley of flavors, including melon, tangerine and Key lime gently drizzled with clover honey."

Uncompahgre Valley Wineries

San Juan Mountain Range south of Olathe

Uncompahgre Valley Wineries

1. Cottonwood Cellars/The Olathe Winery
5482 Colo. Highway 348, Olathe, CO 81425
(970) 323-6224

2. Garrett Estate Cellars
53582 Falcon Road, Olathe, CO 81425
(970) 901-5919

3. Mountain View Winery
5859 58.25 Road, Olathe, CO 81425
(970) 323-6816

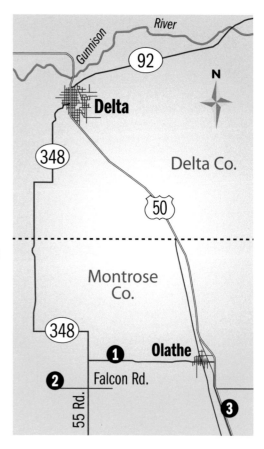

The Uncompahgre Valley has a long history of agriculture

A bountiful land for farming

The river giving this valley its name emerges from the lap of the San Juan Mountains, its birthplace where the waters of creation boil out of the ground.

Higher even, up where the wildflowers cascade like rainbow-hued mantillas from the granite prominence, the winter snows melt and the waters seep and purl into the earth.

Emerging through narrow profiles and deep pools, hot and cold flows mingle and the Uncompahgre River moves on, past tourists swimming and trout finning, where deer and elk and mountain lions come warily to slake their thirst.

The river and its widening valley, bounded south and east by the snag-filled San Juan Mountains and on the west by the staired landscape of the Uncompahgre Plateau, serve as home to livestock growers and orchardists, hay farmers, corn farmers and the oft-conflicting irruption of people attracted to a fertile landscape where wild geese fly and snow-covered mountains peer into their homes.

The word "uncompahgre" is of Ute origin and according to *The Origin of Certain Place Names in the United States* (Henry Gannett, 1846–1914), is a combination of three words: unca (hot), pah (water) and gre (spring).

Reflective of the river's near-constant silt-fogged nature, the name also has been variously translated as meaning "Dirty Water" or "Rocks That Make Water Red."

The water has carried the stories and hopes of multiform peoples since Paleo Indians traversed the region 10,000 years ago. Spanish explorers reached the area in the late 1600s, bringing domestic beasts of burden, including the culture-changing horse, perhaps the most significant of the transitions that continue to this day.

From the narrow defiles above Ouray, the valley expands and spreads, and by 60 miles downstream the mountains provide the backdrop to a fecund alluvial lowland wedged between the sharp ridge hiding the Gunnison River and the stepped mesas of the Uncompahgre Plateau.

This is a farming valley and farming community, from the horse and cattle ranchers to bee farmers, lavender growers and the impenetrable expanses of sweet corn raised on water from the Uncompahgre and Gunnison rivers.

The history of farming is extensive and manifold. As early as the spring of 1882, pioneer rancher and farmer Sam Wade was tending grapevines and numerous fruit trees at his homestead along the nearby North Fork of the Gunnison River.

Farmers quickly learned which areas were best-suited for fruit and today, along with traditional fruit-growing practices, you'll find a handful of winemakers determinedly plying their trade.

Some of the latter are retirees, emigrants curious about the potential of a Colorado wine culture and finding in the Uncompahgre Valley a bountiful land where the scattering of orchards holds forth the promise of a future in grapes.

Some of the winemakers are long-time Uncompahgre Valley families turning their century or more of close-to-the-land energy and attentions to the equally parlous pursuit of tangled vines.

They all are pioneers, daring to leap into a void where the local history of winemaking is being writ with every harvest and every barrel. To them a toast, in equal parts thanks and esteem, for theirs is the continuation of a creative entrepreneurship that finds its voice in each glass of Colorado wine.

The history of farming is extensive and manifold. As early as the spring of 1882, pioneer rancher and farmer Sam Wade was tending grapevines and numerous fruit trees at his homestead along the nearby North Fork of the Gunnison River.

Cottonwood Cellars near Olathe

Cottonwood Cellars: 'It should be a misdemeanor to drink wines too young'

On warm summer afternoons, guests to this winery amidst the farmlands east of Olathe may be forgiven for tarrying a bit longer than planned.

The westerly sun weighs heavy on a sojourner and nothing reanimates like sipping a glass of wine while digging bare toes in the lush green lawn and listening to the leaves whisper softly from the century-old cottonwood trees gracing the front lawn of Cottonwood Cellars.

No mystery how owners Keith and Diana Read named their winery. Three elephantine gray-barked trees, coarse, unironed and enduring, shelter the lawn and throw a canopy of shade over the winery and tasting room.

Just as the stately trees offer bonhomie to the traveler, the Reads also throw open their doors to the

43

thirsty.

And also like one of the guardian cottonwoods whose bifurcated trunk doubles the tree's span, Cottonwood Cellars is two wineries in one.

In addition to the eponymous Cottonwood Cellars label, the Reads also produce wines under The Olathe Winery label.

"It's the same company, same winemaker, same business," explains Diana in a rare quiet moment. "The styles are different and they have a different price point."

The Olathe Winery offers wines that are lighter and more immediately accessible, she says, whereas the Cottonwood Cellars wines tend toward full-bodied Bordeaux- and Burgundian-style wines where a little aging can do wonders.

"We love to age-soften our Bordeaux-style blends," Diana says. "We get emails from people with some of our 1990-something (Cabernet Sauvignon) they inherited and they'll ask if it's still good.

"And then they'll taste and say, 'It's wonderful.' "

"I think it should be a misdemeanor to drink wines too young," she says, a note in her voice assuring a listener she isn't completely kidding.

So sure are the Reads of the power of aging that when the 2012 San Francisco International Wine Competition asked for a bottle of the Cottonwood Cellars 2009 Cabernet Sauvignon, the Reads were reluctant to let it go.

"We wouldn't usually release an '09 that early (in 2013, the 2005 and 2006 vintages were current releases) but we knew it was a very good wine," says Diana.

The wine deemed too young to drink earned a Gold Medal.

The Reads purchased their 52-acre farm in 1989, and planted the first grapes in 1994. Theirs was the first winery in the Olathe area, and the Reads soon discovered location dictated what they could grow.

Keith had experience growing apricots, plums and walnuts in California and when he and Diana left the high-tech world for Western Colorado, his first stop was Ridgway.

"But it was winter and there were 3 feet of snow up there," recalls Diana with a shudder. "I told him, 'I love snow and I love to ski, but I want to go home at night.' "

They settled on their current location after Keith saw the acres of fruit trees in the area, and soon he was taking winemaking lessons from Erik Bruner, the late and talented winemaker for Plum Creek Winery in Palisade.

A skilled researcher, Keith chose Lemberger and Pinot Noir grapes for the farm's 5,400-foot elevation.

"Keith said both Pinot Noir and Lemberger would like the high altitude and cool climate and we've never lost a crop," Diana says. "We have the ideal location for growing Pinot Noir."

In addition to red Pinot Noir and Lemberger, the Reads produce an off-dry white Pinot Noir and off-dry white Lemberger under The Olathe Winery label.

There also is a unique blend they call "Pinolem," a sweeter red wine made for friends and conversation.

"It's for people who are just getting into wine or those who just drink wine, not eat with it," explains Diana.

Cottonwood Cellars' traditional-style dry reds and whites are meant to grace your table alongside Colorado-grown fare.

"Our dry reds are for food in the European style," Diana says. "And particularly food grown in Colorado, like elk, deer, beef, lamb and pork and the abundance of fresh vegetables we find around us."

And visitors soon learn not to ask "What's your best wine?' "

"It's not, 'What's your best wine?' " affirms Diana, as though correcting a wayward child. "It's 'What's for dinner?' That's how we think about our wines."

Cottonwood Cellars/The Olathe Winery

5482 Highway 348, Olathe, CO, 81425-0940
(970) 323-6224;
cottonwoodcellars.com;
winfo@cottonwoodcellars.com
Est.: 1994 **Owners:** Keith and Diana Read
Winemaker: Keith Read **Wines produced:**
Cabernet Sauvignon, Classic Blend, Merlot,
Lemberger, Syrah, Pinot Noir, Gewürztraminer,
White Pinot Noir, Tawny Merlot (Port),
Chardonnay, Pinolem, White Lemberger,
Claret, Reserve Merlot and Reserve Cabernet
Price range: $12 to $39 **Annual production:**
3,500 cases at Cottonwood Cellars and
1,000 cases at The Olathe Winery

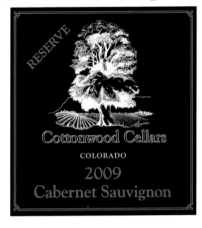

Tasting room: Open Fridays and Saturdays 11 a.m. to 5:30 p.m. April 1 through Memorial
Day weekend, Wednesday through Saturdays 11 a.m. to 5:30 p.m. Memorial Day through
Sept. 30, and Fridays and Saturdays 11 a.m. to 5 p.m. Oct. 1 through Dec. 24. Call on
Monday holidays to confirm open. **Tours:** Yes, when not busy, or upon reservation. **Other
amenities:** Gift shop with T-shirts, sweatshirts and wine-related items including products
made from oak wine barrels. Wine dinners by prior appointment. Events for up to 75
people indoors or 125 outdoors. Picnic grounds in the grass under the cottonwood trees.
Ask for wine club details

Winemaker's choice: "We are known for our Reserve
Cabernet Sauvignon, which pairs well with game, fatty beef
steaks and dark chocolate."

*"We are a family
winery, which started
as Keith's retirement
project and has
grown through
popular demand for
quality wines and his
love of the art."*

Cottonwood Cellars and The Olathe Winery, its label for
lighter-bodied wines, grow 22 acres of vineyards. All wines
are estate-grown except for Cabernet Sauvignon. Grown
on site are Pinot Noir, Merlot, Cabernet Franc, Lemberger,
Chardonnay and Gewürztraminer. Pinot Noir thrives at
altitude, and Cottonwood Cellars consistently harvests 3
tons to the acre. Even in years with challenging weather,
both Pinot Noir and Lemberger make it to harvest.

On the 52-acre farm punctuated with towering, 120-year-old cottonwood trees are three
soil types. Between the soil, high altitude and dry climate, Cottonwood Cellars produces
world-class quality wine as shown through winning international competitions.

In 2012, Cottonwood Cellars won four international awards: Gold, Silver and two
Bronze. The Bordeaux blend in 2011 won the Governor's Cup Best of Show for Red and a
Gold Medal.

The 2009 vintage Cabernet Sauvignon won a Gold Medal at the San Francisco
International Wine Competition.

**"Don't leave our winery without first tasting our White Lemberger,
which tastes like cherries, strawberries and peaches. It makes a
great Sangria!"**

Garrett Estate Cellars

53582 Falcon Road, Olathe, CO 81425;
(970) 901-5919; garrettestatecellars.com;
mitch@garrettestatecellars.com
Est.: 2003 when vines were planted, selling
wines by 2010 **Owners:** Dave and Pamela
Garrett **Wines produced:** Chardonnay,
Pinot Gris, Riesling (dry), Gewürztraminer
(dry), Cabernet Sauvignon, Cabernet Franc,
Pheasant Run Red Blend and Merlot **Price
range:** $10 to $20 **Annual production:**
4,000 cases

Tasting room: Located at Rocking W Cheese and Dairy in Olathe. Open all year from
10 a.m. to 6 p.m. Monday through Saturday. However, special events and winery dinners
will be at the winery. **Tours:** By appointment. **Other amenities:** Artwork from local artists.
Event facility accommodates 30 people. No gift shop, but the winery does have artwork
from local artists.

Winemaker's choice: "Gewürztraminer (dry) with a pork tenderloin covered in an apple/
cinnamon glaze, wild rice infused with diced pecans, and cooked asparagus and carrots
lightly drizzled with a maple syrup sauce."

Garrett Estate Cellars has 35 acres of vineyards with an additional 20 prepared for
planting and more expansion acreage available. Growing now are Chardonnay, Pinot Gris,
Riesling, Gewürztraminer, Cabernet Sauvignon and Merlot. Future plans include planting
Cabernet Franc and a possible hybrid variety. At 5,400 feet in elevation, the soil is rocky
and sandy, with a tiny amount of clay mixed with some alkaline. Temperatures during the
growing season range in the 90s in the daytime to the 60s in the evening. The day to night
temperature swings lock the flavor into the grapes. Garrett Estate Cellars' wines won awards
at numerous wine competitions including international, Arizona, California and Colorado.
Some of those awards are:
2009 Riesling: Governor's Cup — Silver
2010 Sauvignon Blanc: Finger Lakes International Wine Competition — Bronze
2010 Chardonnay: Western Wine Competition (Sonoma, Calif.) — Gold
2009 Gewürztraminer: Florida State International Wine Competition — Silver
2010 Pinot Gris: Colorado Mountain Winefest — Gold
2009 Rosé: Finger Lakes International Wine Competition — Bronze
2011 Viognier: Southwest Wine Competition (Prescott, Ariz.) — Gold
2009 Merlot: FLIWC — Silver
2009 Pheasant Run Red Blend: FLIWC — Silver
2009 Cabernet Sauvignon: Western Wine Competition (Sonoma, Calif.) — Silver
2009 Cabernet Franc: FLIWC — Silver

*"We want to produce great dry wines at a great value — great wines
that happen to be from Colorado."*

"Don't leave our winery without first trying all our wines."

Mountain View Winery

5859 58.25 Road, Olathe, CO 81425;
(970) 323-6816; mountainviewwinery.com;
mountainviewwinery@gmail.com
Est.: 2001 **Owners:** Mike and Wendy Young
Winemaker: Mike Young **Wines produced:**
Traditional red and whites, blends and fruit wine
Price range: $14 to $28 **Annual production:**
1,000 cases
Tasting room: Open 10 a.m. to 6 p.m. Monday
through Saturday year-round. **Tours:** Anytime, as
long as they're not terribly busy. **Other amenities:**
Picnic grounds and room for large events. There's
also a selection of local artisan products from elk sausage to candles and soaps to jewelry.
You-pick fruits and vegetables in season, from March through October, weather permitting.
Ask for wine club details

Winemaker's choice: "Our Uncompahgre is a Cherry/Merlot blend and dry. We love it with
any traditional red wine meal or with pork dishes and even just a salad. "

With the slogan "Flavors of the tree as well as the vine," Mountain View Winery is a multi-generational orchard and vineyard with seasonal fruits and vegetables available for visitors
to pick themselves.

First are the purple-crowned asparagus spears in March and April. Cherries come on
in June, then peaches and pears in August and September. Apples end the season in
September and October.

Mountain View has a natural vineyard of 4.5 acres producing Chardonnay, Riesling,
Gewürztraminer, Merlot, Barbera, Pinot Noir and Pinot Grigio.

Some visitors plan a bicycle tour from Delta or Montrose to the winery.

"We are within a 45-minute drive of Black Canyon
National Park. We'd be honored if you came and
visited our winery during your next visit to our area."

**"Don't leave our winery without first sitting for a spell with a glass
of wine and just enjoy the peaceful surroundings."**

Riesling grapes

North Fork Valley Wineries

Harvest begins at Leroux Creek Vineyards

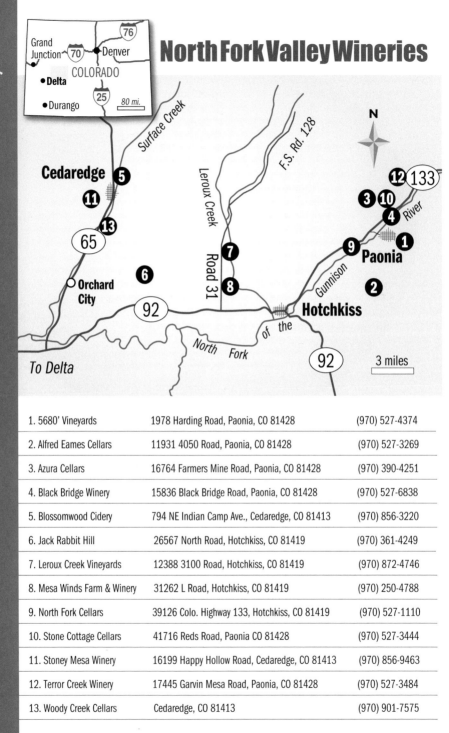

North Fork Valley Wineries

1. 5680' Vineyards	1978 Harding Road, Paonia, CO 81428	(970) 527-4374
2. Alfred Eames Cellars	11931 4050 Road, Paonia, CO 81428	(970) 527-3269
3. Azura Cellars	16764 Farmers Mine Road, Paonia, CO 81428	(970) 390-4251
4. Black Bridge Winery	15836 Black Bridge Road, Paonia, CO 81428	(970) 527-6838
5. Blossomwood Cidery	794 NE Indian Camp Ave., Cedaredge, CO 81413	(970) 856-3220
6. Jack Rabbit Hill	26567 North Road, Hotchkiss, CO 81419	(970) 361-4249
7. Leroux Creek Vineyards	12388 3100 Road, Hotchkiss, CO 81419	(970) 872-4746
8. Mesa Winds Farm & Winery	31262 L Road, Hotchkiss, CO 81419	(970) 250-4788
9. North Fork Cellars	39126 Colo. Highway 133, Hotchkiss, CO 81419	(970) 527-1110
10. Stone Cottage Cellars	41716 Reds Road, Paonia CO 81428	(970) 527-3444
11. Stoney Mesa Winery	16199 Happy Hollow Road, Cedaredge, CO 81413	(970) 856-9463
12. Terror Creek Winery	17445 Garvin Mesa Road, Paonia, CO 81428	(970) 527-3484
13. Woody Creek Cellars	Cedaredge, CO 81413	(970) 901-7575

A passion for the land

Perhaps the best vantage to fathom the magnitude of what the North Fork Valley offers is from the tasting-room veranda at Joan and John Mathewson's Terror Creek Winery, high on a south-facing shoulder of Garvin Mesa and at 6,400 feet elevation possibly the highest winery in the world.

Your eyes initially catch the sweep of mountains, from the volcanic crags and cliffs of lake-pocked Grand Mesa to the snowy peaks of the West Elk Mountains embracing McClure Pass and on to the weather-etched crest of Mount Lamborn towering across the valley.

Through the heart of this high-country splendor slips the meandering trace of the North Fork of the Gunnison River, along which are spread the emerald-like fields, orchards and vineyards that cause some viewers to proclaim this fertile valley "An American Provence."

In his 2011 book of that same name, Colorado geography professor and writer Thomas Huber suggested the two valleys, though separated by thousands of miles, could be "twins — fraternal twins."

"If a person were to close their eyes, they could not tell if they were in Provence or the North Fork Valley," writes Huber.

And although these twins may speak different languages, they share even more — the light, the climate, the agriculture and the people with a passion for the land on which they live.

Since the 1880s the North Fork Valley has been a workingman's valley, where ranchers, farmers and coal miners carved out an existence in a less-traveled part of Colorado.

While those endeavors continue to help define the North Fork Valley, since the 1970s, as the trickle of tourists discovering Colorado grew to a deluge, a new vibrancy has taken hold.

A growing interest in sustainable and organic agriculture found a welcome home in the North Fork Valley, and visitors today find a multitude of organic gardens, vineyards and orchards supplanting

West Elk Mountains from Terror Creek Winery near Paonia

traditional methods of raising food and farm animals.

In an unexpected divination of today's flowering wine industry, the area was selected as part of the 1970s-era Four Corners Project, an effort across Western Colorado, Utah, New Mexico and Arizona to see where wine grapes might be grown successfully and profitably.

More than 20 years before Tom Huber limned poetic about this valley's semblance to the rich wine country of France, nascent winemakers explored for themselves the promising bounty of fertile soils, plentiful water and abundant sunshine under iris-blue skies.

Today, there are 16 wineries in the North Fork /Delta region, 11 of which are in the North Fork-centric West Elks American Viticultural Area, one of two designated AVAs in the state.

Individually and collectively, the wineries offer a medley of wines in a range of styles, denoting the individualism found in small, owner-operated wineries.

You will discover educated and perceptive winemakers devoted to bottling a dream while retaining that ineffable sense of place tying together the land, the people and their wines.

Azura Cellars near Paonia

5680' Vineyards

1978 Harding Road, Paonia, CO 81428; (970) 527-4374 (tasting room) (970) 527-6470 (winery); 5680vineyards@gmail.com
Est.: 2005 **Owner and Winemaker:** Rob Kimball **Wines produced:** Pinot Noir, Syrah, Chardonnay, Elevation Red and dessert **Price range:** $15 to $20 **Annual production:** 500 cases
Tasting room: Located at the Fresh & Wyld Farmhouse Inn, 1978 Harding Road in Paonia. To hold an event featuring 5680' Vineyards' wines, call the Fresh & Wyld Farmhouse Inn at (970) 527-4374.

Winemaker's choice: "Our Syrah Dessert Wine pairs well with a lounge chair and a cigar."

Owner and winemaker Rob Kimball has three vineyards producing Pinot, Syrah and Chardonnay grapes at 5,680 feet above sea level. In this thin air, piercing sunlight ripens the fruit, but a crisp acidity is preserved.

Rob respects the natural process that transforms grapes to wine with minimal intervention. Every wine reflects what the vineyard offered in a particular year.

"5680' Vineyards is a one-man, one-dog operation."

"Don't leave our winery without first scratching the dog's head."

Alfred Eames Cellars

11931 4050 Road,
Paonia, CO 81428;
(970) 527-3269;
alfredeamescellars.com;
eames@paonia.com
Est.:1995 **Owner and Winemaker:** Alfred Eames Petersen **Wines produced:** Pinot Noir, Syrah, Tempranillo, Port and three blends **Price range:** $18 to $25
Annual production: 1,500 cases
Tasting room: Tastings on occasion. **Tours:** By appointment and during special events. **Other amenities:** Visitors are welcome to picnic by the pond.

Winemaker's choice:
"I love them all and will pair them with just about anything."

Alfred Eames Petersen has been making wine for some 45 years. Now, 3 miles south of Paonia in the West Elks American Viticultural Area, he grows 3 acres of Pinot Noir grapes, with a few other varieties scattered about.

The high altitude — 5,959 feet — and soils contribute to good acid content. The rugged weather, he believes, gives character to the grapes that survive.

The barrel cellar is an underground double vault imagined and built to function like a cave. In it, red wines are fermented in open vats and barrel aged in French oak, unfined and unfiltered. White wines are barrel fermented and lightly filtered.

"Don't leave our winery without first spending time tasting wine."

Azura Cellars

16764 Farmers Mine Road, Paonia, CO 81428; (970) 390-4251; azuracellars.com; azurapaonia@aol.com **Est.:** 2006 **Owners:** Ty and Helen Gillespie **Winemaker:** Ty Gillespie **Wines produced:** Cabernet Sauvignon, Syrah, Yacht Club Red (a blend), Pinot Gris and Riesling **Price range:** All wines are $20 **Annual production:** 200 cases **Tasting room:** A fine art gallery featuring the Gillespies' sculptures doubles as a tasting room, open from 11 a.m. to 6 p.m. Memorial Day through the end of October. **Tours:** On request. **Other amenities:** Picnic grounds on the terrace. Azura Yacht Club Wednesday evenings. Weddings for up to 40 people.

Winemaker's choice: "Our Riesling pairs very nicely with spicy Thai food."

Colorado may be landlocked, but a sailboat inspired the name of Azura Cellars. Boats even can be seen, in remote control version, bobbing along high-country waves.

Sailors, artists and winemakers Ty and Helen Gillespie sailed around the world for six years on their 38-foot sailboat, Azura, before landing ashore their Colorado mountain home. On Wednesday evenings, the Gillespies and their guests sail RC sailboats at the "Azura Yacht Club."

"Our gallery offers world-class, contemporary fine art we created ourselves."

"Don't leave our winery without first lingering to enjoy our view of the West Elk Mountains and the North Fork Valley from our terrace."

Black Bridge Winery

15836 Black Bridge Road, Paonia, CO 81428;
(970) 527-6838; blackbridgewinery.com;
leeb@orchardvalleyfarms.com

Est.: 2004 **Owners:** Lee and Kathy Bradley
Winemaker: Lee Bradley **Wines produced:** Pinot
Noir, Merlot, Chardonnay, red blends, dessert wines,
Rosé and Riesling **Price range:** $16 to $25 **Annual
production:** 1,500 cases

Tasting room: Open 10 a.m. to 6 p.m. daily,
Memorial Day weekend through Halloween. **Tours:**
By appointment. **Other amenities:** Picnic area and
event facilities for up to 50 people. Orchard Valley
Farms & Market sells fruits and vegetables grown
on site and other locally crafted foods, such as
chocolate wine sauce, jams, jellies and salsas.
Ask for wine club details

Winemaker's choice: "Our Pinot Noir goes with
anything — it is very versatile. It really pairs well with
pasta dishes."

Black Bridge Winery takes its name from the century-old bridge
spanning the Gunnison River just out the front door. Set among
acres of gardens and orchards, the winery's vineyards are planted
in Pinot Noir, Merlot, Chardonnay and Riesling. Soil is a stony
loam. Cool nights and warm days produce tart, fruity (not flabby)
Chardonnay and Riesling grapes.

A striking 85-foot-long wine cave — the site of winemaking and
barrel-tasting events — is ribbed with steel recycled from an old
mining operation in the area. Handmade doors and rockwork on
the cave entrance complete the artful repurposing and blending
of traditional and new industries of the North Fork region.

Wine is aged in oak barrels in the wine cave for 16 months.
The naturally controlled underground temperature ranges from 40
degrees in winter to 60 degrees in summer.

Black Bridge's 2008 Pinot won Double Gold at the 2010 Colorado Mountain Winefest. At the Colorado Governor's Cup awards, the 2009 Pinot and
2011 Chardonnay won Silver in 2012, and the 2008 Pinot and 2009 Riesling
won Bronze in 2010.

*"We are a
family-owned
farm and
winery with
our roots in
agriculture."*

**"Don't leave our winery without first touring our orchards and
vineyards. You can pick your own fruit and veggies."**

Blossomwood Cidery

794 NE Indian Camp Ave., Cedaredge,
CO 81413; (970) 856-3220;
blossomwoodcidery.com
info@blossomwoodcidery.com

Est.: 2006 **Owners:** Shawn and Janese Carney
Cidermaker: Shawn Carney **Cider produced:**
Traditional French-style cider, and blends
from a mix of English, French and American
cider apples **Price range:** $7 to $9 **Annual
production:** 2,000 cases

Tasting room: Open from noon to 4 p.m. June
to November and off-season by appointment.
Tours: By request during tasting room hours.
Other amenities: Picnic areas in the orchard
and on a covered patio. Gift shop with apple
products made on site such as Boiled Cider,
as it is called in New England, which is a pure
apple syrup, and Le Niere Beurre, or Jersey Black Butter,
which is a type of French apple butter originally from the
Isle of Jersey.

Cidermaker's choice: "Our traditional English Perry
is a rare treat since there are less than 100 acres of
traditional Perry pears in the entire U.S. It is mellow,
fruity and has a touch of astringency. Food would
probably distract from its enjoyment."

"We enjoy talking about traditional cider with other enthusiasts. For people who are thinking about cider as a career, we take an enthusiastic role in working with other producers in the Colorado cider industry."

Blossomwood Cidery raises mostly French cider
varieties: Bramtot, Muscadet de Dieppe, Muscadet de
Bernay, Medaille D'or and Frequin Rouge. The 15-acre
orchard includes old standing and new high-density
cider trees.

It is truly a rare and unique collection of cider apple
and pear varieties from around the world. The international flair continues in the gift shop,
with traditional products that normally would only be available in Europe.

Blossomwood is one of the few U.S. producers using a European process called keeving.
Still practiced in Normandy, keeving is a technique that preserves the natural sugars in the
apple juice, yielding a semi-sweet product without adding juice or sugar at bottling.

The cider-specific pears, called Perry pears in Europe, have shown to be more
dependent on the soil type than the apples. Blossomwood gets high tannin levels and rich
flavors from its estate Perry cider.

**"Don't leave our cidery without first learning about our estate
nursery where we propagate and grow all our own trees of rare and
unusual varieties that will be planted in our cider orchards."**

Jack Rabbit Hill: 'We go to the customer'

Jack Rabbit Hill Winery really isn't *that* hard to find.

Sure, it's sort of in the middle of Redlands Mesa and the two-track lane does get a bit slick and there aren't a whole lot of signs, but that's so you can savor the view from the courtly home on what is, yes, Jack Rabbit Hill.

Besides, it's not like Anna and Lance Hanson, hands-on owners and operators of the winery and accompanying Peak Spirits Distillery, aren't aware of their, well, pastoral location.

"I've had people say, 'Are you with the CIA? We're trying so hard to find you, do you not want to be found?'" Anna says with a laugh, even though such words probably aren't what most small business owners like to hear.

Still, visitors successful in their search will be pleased there isn't a long line outside the tasting room, which most of the time serves as the Hansons' soul-bracing kitchen, where you gaze out broad picture windows

at the biodynamic vineyards and a comforting sweep of Colorado sky.

How two Bay Area refugees wound up in Western Colorado with a winery and a distillery with a James Beard award nomination is a novel recount of people visiting Colorado on vacation, liking what they see, and digging in their claws.

The Hansons were visiting relatives when they found themselves hooked on the land and the people and soon decided this was their path.

"Now, I can't imagine doing anything else," says Lance, ever the optimist.

Their first augury that a winery was a wise decision came a year later.

"We had a real tiny harvest in 2002 and finally made our first wine," recalls Lance. "There wasn't much, maybe a barrel each of white and red, and the following summer in June we were at the Aspen farmers market and sold our first bottle.

"We couldn't believe someone would

Jack Rabbit Hill on Redlands Mesa

pay for it. That was a huge milestone."

From potential millstone to milestone, all it took was a little love from what can be a very selective audience.

Today, they laugh at the naiveté displayed by two big-city escapees seeking a better life for their young family.

"The original plan was to grow grapes here in this beautiful spot and try to create something interesting we could sell into the Colorado market," says Lance. "If you would have asked me back then, I would have said my original agenda was do a vineyard and wines on a much larger scale.

"We had two young kids at the time; we had to do something that would work."

What works, they found out, is being who they are.

"Our story about how and why we farm the way we do, and what it translates into in terms of quality resonated with restaurant buyers," Lance says. "Even though our wine production was very, very small, we realized there was something here interesting to these people."

That small production and their location well off the main road made their next decision that much easier — adopting what Lance calls the "outbound approach."

"We go to the customer rather than waiting for the customer to come to us," he says.

Today, Jack Rabbit Hill's biodynamic and organic wines are served at top restaurants in Colorado and elsewhere.

"We bring restaurant groups up to the farm and they stay for the weekend, see what we're doing up here, and they fall in love with it," says Anna. "They become our best sales force."

Peak Spirits Distillery, with its James Beard Award-winning CapRock Gin, was a natural extension of the winery.

"I have to say the distillery worked perfectly, a real easy transition," says Anna. "It was a very natural thing to get into."

Only locally organically grown fruit and crystal-pure water from a high-mountain spring go into their CapRock Gin, Vodka and Peak Spirits European-style grappa and eau de vies.

"Before we started the distillery the winters were kind of slow," muses Lance. "But that's not true anymore.

"Now, it seems we're always behind. But if we didn't grow grapes on the property, it wouldn't be anywhere near as interesting."

Lance Hanson, co-owner
of Jack Rabbit Hill

Jack Rabbit Hill

26567 North Road, Hotchkiss, CO 81419; (970) 361-4249; jackrabbithill.com; anna@jackrabbithill.com
Est.: 2001 **Owners and winemakers:** Anna and Lance Hanson **Wines produced:** Pinot Noir, Meunier, Riesling, Chardonnay, Foch and Vignoles. Also home to Peak Spirits Farm Distillery, maker of CapRock Gin
Price range: $18 to $28 **Annual production:** 1,500 cases
Tastings and tours: By appointment. **Other amenities:** Picnic grounds. Check website for farm dinners schedule.
Ask for wine club details

Jack Rabbit Hill™

M&N 2011

58% Pinot Noir, 42% Pinot Meunier
Grown At Jack Rabbit Hill Farm
Certified Biodynamic®
13.7% alc by vol
Colorado

Winemaker's choice: "The 2011 M&N (Pinot Noir/Meunier blend) paired with spring lamb grown at Jack Rabbit Hill!"

Jack Rabbit Hill is a 70-acre diversified farm operation that is Demeter biodynamic certified. With a tagline of "Healing the planet through agriculture," Demeter Association Inc. encourages biodynamic practices that treat the farm as a living organism. Livestock, wildlife and agriculture co-exist, and at least 10% of farmland is set aside as a biodiversity preserve.

That meant integrating sheep, cattle, chickens and bees into Jack Rabbit Hill's 17-acre vineyard, 10-acre hopyard and other farmlands. The farm was always organic, but since adopting biodynamic practices, Jack Rabbit Hill was able to reduce compost needs to 30% of what was required before, and the soil quality is better. Continued certification requires annual inspection.

"The biodynamic standard helps us use the farm's own natural assets to grow better, more expressive fruit with a lighter footprint than conventional or other organic standards."

Jack Rabbit Hill's wines have received a 2012 James Beard Nomination and the Edible Aspen Magazine Artisan Beverage Producer of the Year in 2010 and 2009.

Leroux Creek Vineyards northwest of Hotchkiss

Leroux Creek Vineyards: 'You would swear you are in Provence'

It started here, all that talk about Colorado's North Fork Valley being the American Provence.

Writer and geographer Thomas Huber duly gets official credit for first publicly coining the expression of twin-ness between the North Fork Valley and the Provence region of France 5,000 miles away, but he wasn't the first person to notice the similarity.

That honor, we presume, belongs to Yvon Gros and his wife, Joanna Reckert, who at first sight felt an early kinship with their future home along Leroux Creek.

What they encountered in this Colorado mountain valley in 1999 was a heart-stopping iteration of that far-distant area where Yvon spent his younger years.

"Oh, yes, we saw it right away," says Yvon, sitting on the greenery-wrapped deck of the Leroux Creek Inn, a well-popped cork's distance from the lush vineyards that supply his winery. "You look across the fields at the mesa over there and you would swear you are in Provence."

The sage-and-juniper-dotted land was rougher, without the orderly vineyards now gracing the view from the well-appointed Southwest-style inn highlighted by Joanna's elegant touch.

But they saw promise enough to give them pause, says Joanna, who back then had just finished a bike trip through Provence.

"When we saw this place, we knew," she says. "I mean, I'd just been to Provence and it was like, 'I think we're home.'"

Yvon was raised near Lac d'Annecy in northwest France and spent many summers in Provence and he, too, immediately recognized the connection between the North Fork Valley and the rural France of his youth. His mother's family had a dairy farm, his father an affineur (cheese finisher) in Provence.

"I'd spend summers with my mother's family on their dairy farm and this is just like that," a hint of wonder evident in his voice. "On my second trip here, the sun was out and I looked around and said, 'We have to have this place.' "

Yvon says Thomas Huber, whose mother-in-law was from Provence, had his inspiration one early morning in 2003.

"He was just back from Provence and he was staying in that room, right up there," says Yvon, pointing at the second-story window overlooking the valley. "And one morning he came down to breakfast, and said, 'You won't believe this, but I just had the feeling I was looking out at Provence.' "

Yvon laughed in delight.

"We told him, 'You aren't so crazy, we saw it, too.' "

Some might call their vision a gamble, but it's only a gamble when you might not win.

"I knew the farm would grow good grapes," Yvon says. "The climate is similar, the soil is volcanic, different but very good."

Today Leroux Creek Inn is a sun-splashed bed and breakfast reflecting Joanna's intimate knowledge of design and where Yvon showcases his wines and his lifelong culinary skills, fine-tuned at the Thonon-les-Bains Cooking School.

"My first love is cooking," he affirms. "My mother was a great cook and she always had me in the kitchen. I got my technique from school, of course, but so much of my cooking now is from my mother."

Yvon and Joanna, who developed a signature line of grape-seed-based skin-care products, expanded the original vineyard and among Leroux Creek's wines today are Chambourcin, an aromatic, deep-colored red wine, and Cayuga, a crisp white wine with floral and fruit notes similar to Riesling.

The cold-hardy hybrid grapes were chosen for their ability to express the particular terroir of the North Fork Valley.

"When people say terroir they think it's just the soil, but it's so much more than that," says Yvon of his organic farming, which includes vinegar for weed control and horse manure for fertilizer.

He crosses his arms, exuding c'est la bonne façon, that what he and Joanna are sharing is right for themselves, their inn and their wines.

"It's the climate, it's the people, it's the dogs and the horses and everybody is a part of it all," he says with a grin. "It makes me excited about the new season."

Yvon Gros, co-owner of Leroux Creek Vineyards

Leroux Creek Vineyards

12388 3100 Road, Hotchkiss, CO 81419; (970) 872-4746; lerouxcreekinn.com; info@lerouxcreekinn.com

Est.: 2000 **Owners:** Joanna Reckert and Yvon Gros **Winemaker:** Yvon Gros **Wines produced:** French and American hybrids. Dry wines as well as sweet dessert wines **Price range:** $12.50 to $25 **Annual production:** 500 to 600 cases

Tasting room: Open from 11 a.m. to 5 p.m. April through the end of October. **Tours:** By appointment May through October. **Other amenities:** The gift shop carries an organic line of skincare products made from grape-seed oil and grapes. French classic food includes local and French cheeses, Charcuterie (Prosciutto, dried sausage and dried meat), and crudités (French salads made with local produce) – just right for enjoying on the picnic grounds. Events for up to 100.

Winemaker's choice: "Cayuga white is a light wine with apricot tones and good balance that will pair well with a local smoked trout."

"We are a small winery and love to share our love for the vineyard and winemaking with our guests, I, Yvon, am from the French Alps and studied the culinary arts and enology in France, and my wife, Joanna, is a clothing designer from New York City. We have both been in Colorado over 30 years and love it!"

Leroux Creek Vineyards grows 4 acres of hybrids – Chambourcin red and Cayuga white – in volcanic soil at 6,000 feet. Good water, dry weather and cover crops help with pest control in the organic vineyards.

As spectacular as the views on the 52-acre site is the sumptuous food. Owner and winemaker Yvon Gros is trained in French Classic Cuisine and studied at the Thonon-les-Bains Cooking School in Savoie, France. There is open-air dining under a tent overlooking the vineyard, and winemakers dinners and special events.

Leroux Creek wines have won Double Gold, Gold, Silver and Bronze medals at The Finger Lakes International Competition in New York State, Colorado Mountain Winefest in Palisade, The Governor's Cup, and the People's Choice Award at the Ouray Wine & Chocolate Festival.

"Don't leave our winery without first seeing our vineyard and inn, tasting our Aprés Vous, and meeting our wine dogs: Bon Bon, Piaf and Noodle!"

Mesa Winds Farm & Winery

31262 L Road, Hotchkiss, CO 81419;
(970) 250-4788; mesawindsfarm.com;
mail@mesawindsfarm.com
Est.: 2010 **Owners/Winemakers:** Wink Davis
and Max Eisele **Wines produced:** Pinot Gris,
Pinot Meunier, Rosé and Peach **Price range:** $13
to $19 **Annual production:** 450 cases
Tasting room: Open 11 a.m. to 6 p.m. on
Saturdays and Sundays Memorial Day through
mid-October and additional times for special
events. **Tours:** By appointment. **Other amenities:**
Fresh fruit available for purchase during harvest.

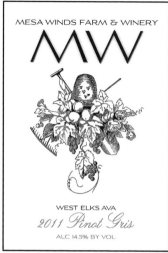

Winemaker's choice: "Folks say our wines
are enjoyable to sip without food pairings,
but I always recommend our Rosé for summer
luncheons. It is best when lunching outside in
pleasant surroundings. Serve it cold with salads, open-
face sandwiches and fruity desserts."

Mesa Winds' vineyards and farm are located in the
heart of Rogers Mesa's organic peach, apple and pear
orchards. Near mesa top, they have a gorgeous view of
the West Elks mountain range.

There are 5 acres of Pinot Noir, Pinot Gris and Pinot
Meunier, and a smattering of Chambourcin grapes,
along with 5.5 acres of organic peaches.

Soils are similar in composition to the soils of
winegrowing regions in France where some of the best
whites are produced. The climate is different from the
Grand Valley AVA, which grows more Mediterranean-
style grapes. The West Elks AVA produces better cool-
weather wines such as Pinots and Rieslings.

*"We enjoy telling people
about our farming and
winemaking practices.
During grape harvest
the atmosphere is
festive and fun, and we
celebrate our harvest
with an evening feast
for our volunteer helpers
— wine included, of
course!"*

Mesa Winds fruit is certified organic. All wines are estate bottled and express the
North Fork Valley's terroir and characteristics. What makes Mesa Winds' wine special is
the where and how the grapes are grown: high altitude, delicately cool nights and hot, dry
days.

Vines are irrigated with clear mountain snowmelt and attended by abundant beneficial
insects.

**"Don't leave our winery without first asking about our farmstays.
We have accommodations for a family or two in our '70s rehabbed
picker cabins. More information about our farmstays is located at
our website. We don't ask people to work on our farm unless they
make that request."**

North Fork Cellars: 'There's been a real revival in hard cider'

The question arises: Why a cidery in a book about wines?

Fair enough. The difference is the fruit, not the process. Apples are crushed, pressed, the juice fermented, voilá.

And we may owe it to John Chapman, known better as Johnny Appleseed, the itinerant nurseryman bare-footing through the Midwest in the early 1800s planting apple orchards.

The mundane among us will point out having a few apple trees was good for real estate sales, but apple trees provided more than fiscal security.

Life could be dreary, and unpasteurized cider, which when stored without refrigeration soon becomes hard cider, was a way to retain the piquancy of summer all year long.

"Europeans have been drinking hard cider for centuries but Prohibition killed it for us," says Jeff Schwartz, co-owner with his wife, Tracey, and brother, Seth, of North Fork Cellars, Delicious Orchards and Big B's Fabulous Juices, the underpinning of this whole story.

Seeking a life closer to the land and suited to their talents and temperaments, Jeff and Tracey moved to Paonia in 2000, and in 2003 partnered with Seth to purchase Big B's in Hotchkiss, a few miles down valley.

In 2006 they purchased what morphed into Delicious Orchards Farm Market, adding to the you-pick orchard a country market and restaurant selling local wines and locally grown meats, cheeses, produce and Big B's organic juices.

In 2010 Shawn Larson came on as their head cider maker, allowing Jeff more time in the orchard.

Shawn, lured away from a job at a specialty food store in Salt Lake City, realized Big B's/Delicious Orchards had everything they needed to make hard apple cider.

"It was kind of a no-brainer," says Shawn, an experienced home brewer who also made hard apple cider at home, of exploiting the store's unsold fresh cider, which would ferment once past the sell-by date. "We already had the (winery) license because of the tasting room and we had plenty of juice, so we went to work perfecting the product."

"In the last few years there's been a real revival in hard cider in the U.S.," he says, referring to the recent entry of major-label beer makers into the cider market.

"But it's like wine or beer," Shawn points out. "There are the mass producers and then there are small-batch artisanal producers making a product they are proud to share.

"There's an increased interest in natural, locally grown food and our cider is part of that trend," Tracey says. "People want to know who grew this, where was it produced. And we can say, 'We did, right here.' "

Tasting room just south of Paonia

North Fork Cellars at Delicious Orchards

39126 Highway 133,
Hotchkiss, CO 81419;
(970) 527-1110;
drinklocally.com;
info@drinklocally.com
Est.: 2008 **Owners:** the
Schwartz family **Cider
maker:** Shawn Larson
Produce: Hard apple
cider **Price range:**
$10 to $25 **Annual
production:** 7,000 cases
Tasting room: Open

daily 9 a.m. to 6 p.m. May through December. **Tours:** Regularly available. **Other amenities:**
A farm store features wares by local artisans and fresh-picked produce, such as sweet
corn, peaches and roasted green chiles. There are picnic grounds and a campground. A
café offers breakfast and lunch, with a variety of soups, salads and sandwiches.

Much of the century-old, 16-acre orchard behind Delicious Orchards Farm Market has
been replanted since 2006, with more changes on the way. Now there are apricot and
cherry trees and recent plantings of Fuji, Gala and Honeycrisp apples. But Jeff Schwartz
has plans for "New World Cider," adding 600 new trees of historical varieties such as
Newtown Pippin and Keystone Black.

Americans are becoming more and more familiar with traditional hard ciders.

Apple cider usually means fresh-pressed, unpasteurized apple juice; any cider with more
than .15% ABV (alcohol by volume) is considered hard cider, which typically range from 6
percent to 8% ABV.

North Fork Cellars' hard cider is vibrant, with its light perlage, crisp fresh-apple flavors
and low alcohol levels.

To meet an expanding hard cider market, in 2013 North Fork Cellars doubled its
production to nearly 7,000 gallons.

The Schwartz family also runs Big B's Fabulous Juices, which has been pressing fresh-
from-the-tree organic juice for 40 years.

Visitors are invited to picnic and camp under the orchard's shady canopy.

*"Guests can come by and hand-pick organic
cherries, pears, peaches and apples."*

**"Don't leave North Fork Cellars without first strolling
through our orchards and enjoying a picnic lunch."**

Stone Cottage Cellars north of Paonia

Stone Cottage Cellars: 'It was a lifestyle we wanted to show our kids'

The whirlpool of wineries claiming to be "a family operation" would dismay Odysseus.

However, on a shoulder of Garvin Mesa near Paonia, with the valley of the North Fork of the Gunnison River 600 feet below, you find the genuine article.

At Stone Cottage Cellars, Brent and Karen Helleckson chose family over careers and found contentment.

It wasn't originally planned as a Laura Ingalls Wilder winemaking refuge, of course, but sometimes in life luck plays as big a role as good intentions.

And when you have both, well ...

The Hellecksons were deep into the high-tech scene in Boulder — Brent an aerospace engineer and Karen a computer technology marketing specialist — when a growing family reminded Brent and Karen of the really important things.

"When we moved here we simply wanted to be out of the city and back in the country," says Brent, his face framed by the familiar dark-blond straw hat.

"We also wanted to spend more time with our kids and this has allowed us to do that," says Karen, finishing his

thought.

They do that, spiraling together sentences and thoughts and building on conversations like a caduceus of design and intent.

They discovered Paonia in 1992 when driving home to Boulder after a raft trip down the Gunnison River.

A stop at a local farm market for apples also produced a real estate brochure "just in case we ever came back here," Karen says.

In 1994 the Hellecksons, both from Midwest farm country, recalled that distant valley with its "beautiful mountains and river and active community," Karen recalls.

It was love at first sight of the untended vineyard on Garvin Mesa, but the dream spot initially proved elusive.

"It was bizarre," says Brent, still a bit of wonder in his voice two decades later. "The property was too much and we couldn't afford it."

But fate twisted, not for the last time.

"When we got home, there was a message on the machine that they dropped the price, so we came back,"

67

Brent says.

Fate? Also staying at the same bed and breakfast was the president of a local bank, who listened to the Hellecksons' dream.

"He said: 'Come on down tomorrow. I know it's Saturday, but I'll have the manager of the bank come down and we'll write up the note,' " says Brent.

"By the end of the weekend we had a vineyard."

The vineyard needed replanting, and there was a home, tasting room and winery to be built, but the Hellecksons had found their future.

"It was a lifestyle we wanted to show our kids," says Karen. "We saw that if we continued doing technology field jobs in Boulder, our kids couldn't be a part of that.

"This was way for us to involve our kids day-to-day in what we were doing."

Brent laughs now at memories of sharing with his family long days digging post holes, planting grapes and wrestling out of the ground the volcanic rocks that he turned into Stone Cottage Cellars.

The initial plan didn't include winemaking, but soon they realized just growing the grapes wasn't enough.

Brent took courses from the renowned winemaking school at University of California-Davis, sought advice from friends and local winemakers, and tackled the staff at the nearby Colorado State University Research Station.

They replanted the 4.5-acre vineyard with Gewürztraminer, Riesling and Chardonnay and a cool-climate variety of Merlot, a family favorite.

"Customers always ask us, 'Are these grown here, are these from Colorado?' " says Karen. "That seems to be more important to the consumer."

"That's part of what makes us different,"

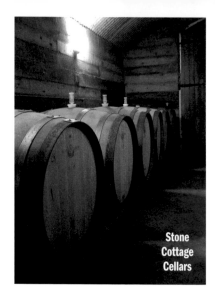

Stone Cottage Cellars

Brent affirms. "We can say, 'Yes, it's grown in Colorado and yes, almost all of them are grown right here and yes, I pruned them or Karen picked them.' "

Today, their success is measured in many ways. The vineyard is healthy, wine production is up, and Brent is building a new home on their land.

That family lifestyle?

"Well, our labor pool is going to college and we have another 600 cases of wine to sell," says Karen with another laugh. "We can't stop now."

Merlot grapes at Stone Cottage Cellars

Stone Cottage Cellars

41716 Reds Road, Paonia,
CO 81428; (970) 527-3444;
stonecottagecellars.com;
info@stonecottagecellars.com
Est.: 2003 **Owners:** Brent
and Karen Helleckson
Winemaker: Brent
Helleckson **Wines produced:**
Gewürztraminer, Chardonnay,
Merlot, Syrah and Pinot Noir
Price range: $20 to $26
Annual production: 1,000
cases
Tasting room: Open from
11 a.m. to 6 p.m. every day
from Memorial Day weekend
through the end of October.
Tours: Guided and self-guided tours of the vineyard are
available upon request. A tour of the cellar also can be
arranged. **Other amenities:** Picnic grounds.

Winemaker's choice: "Our Syrah pairs perfectly with fresh
bread and smoked gouda cheese."

There are 4.5 acres of vineyards at Stone Cottage Cellars
that produce Chardonnay, Merlot, Gewürztraminer and Pinot
Noir. The wines created from these grapes require very little
manipulation and pair well with food. Soils are limestone
marl overlain by volcanic clay, providing access to both the
fertility and nuances produced by volcanic soils and the
limestone characteristics of the great Chardonnay and Pinot
vineyards of the world.

Stone Cottage Cellars has, over the past decade, won
numerous Gold, Silver and Bronze medals at Colorado
Mountain Winefest. Stone Cottage wines have been served,
by invitation, at several prestigious venues including the
Telluride Wine Festival. The initial release of estate-bottled
Chardonnay garnered a score of 87 from *Wine Spectator.*

*"The setting of
our tasting room,
the ambiance
of our wood-
fired oven and
the quality and
uniqueness of our
wine combine to
offer a relaxing,
renewing,
memorable
experience. We
invite you to join
us."*

**"Don't leave our winery without first standing in the vineyard and
drinking in the view."**

Stoney Mesa Winery/Ptarmigan Vineyards

16199 Happy Hollow Road,
Cedaredge, CO 81413;
(970) 856-9463;
stoneymesa.com;
wine@stoneymesa.com

Est.: 1990 **Owner and winemaker:** Bret Neal

Wines produced: Red Blend (Rojo Del Mesa), White Blend (Blanca Del Mesa), Cabernet Sauvignon, Merlot, Pinot Gris, Gewürztraminer, Rosé, Riesling, Late Harvest Muscat (Glacier), Port and Pinot Noir **Price range:** $13 to $30 **Annual production:** 2,500 cases

Tasting room: Open 11 a.m. to 5 p.m. year-round **Tours:** Year-round **Other amenities:** Gift shop with Colorado food products. Events for up to 50 people.

Ask for wine club details

Winemaker's choice: "The Riesling pairs nicely with spicy foods."

Bret Neal of Stoney Mesa Winery grows 9 acres of Chardonnay, Merlot, Gewürztraminer, Baco Noir and Zweigelt.

His wines have garnered Gold medals at the Critics Challenge, the Colorado Mountain Winefest and the Mesa County Fair. They've also won multiple Silver and Bronzes for competitions including the Los Angeles International Wine Competition, Finger Lakes International, Colorado Governor's Cup, Tasters Guild International, IWWC Sonoma, Southwest Wine Competition, Eastern International Wine Competition, Indy International Wine Competition, Next Generation Wine Competition in San Francisco, San Diego National Wine Competition and IWWC San Francisco.

"The passion I have for winemaking is evident in every bottle produced!"

"Don't leave our winery without first coming in and tasting our wine and enjoying our beautiful view of the vineyard."

Terror Creek:
'Pinot Noir is perfect for up here'

The view from the top is marvelous indeed.

"Top" being relative, of course, but in the world of winemaking, Terror Creek Winery, perched at an ear-popping 6,417 feet, indeed is at the apex of the art.

The lovingly tended red-roofed buildings at the end of the unpaved, arrow-straight lane are thought to be the highest winery and vineyard complex in the world, and co-owner/winemaker Joan Mathewson isn't about to argue.

"I really think we're still the highest, although I've heard there are some new vineyards in Argentina that are awfully high," says Joan, one of the first woman winemakers in Colorado.

In spite of its location, or perhaps because of it, Joan's thought when first seeing the vineyards in 1982 with her husband, John, was, "It's really beautiful here and I can't turn this one down."

"Oh, we looked at a lot of property over the years and this one was ideal in many ways," says Joan, preparing herself for the challenges of making wine at unprecedented elevation. "I thought I would just make use of what I have up here."

Terror Creek Winery, named after a nearby stream, kneels high on Garvin Mesa near Paonia, offering visitors stunning views across the North Fork Valley and the horizon-reaching sweep of the West Elk Mountains, where Mount Lamborn and Land's End Peak dominate the near skyline.

The success the Mathewsons have had in growing grapes and making wines at altitude is a credit both to their talent and their desire.

Joan was a self-confessed "ski bum" in Aspen in the 1950s, attended Colorado Women's College, married John (a student at Colorado School of Mines) and traveled with him as his career took him to stops in Europe and Africa.

They both fell in love with Alsatian-style wines, light, elegant and dry, and while John was in Tunisia, Joan went north, working in European vineyards and earning an enology degree at the Engineering School of Enology at Changins, Switzerland.

"There were about 30 men in that class and only two women," she recalls. "Normally in Europe after you get your

Terror Creek Winery

degree you're supposed to be a slave for a while but I didn't have that chance.

"It would have been fun to work under one of the great winemakers but it was matter of moving back to the U.S."

When the Mathewsons bought what eventually would become Terror Creek Winery, they found a few remnant vines, some of them left over from the Four Corners research project of the early 1970s, an attempt to see which grape varieties would grow in plots scattered across Western Colorado, Utah, New Mexico and Arizona.

Most of the vines had succumbed to the years, but a few Gewürztraminer vines and even some Cabernet Sauvignon were alive, Joan says.

"The Cabernet Sauvignon grew nicely but never would get ripe," she says. "In Colorado, it never has time to get ripe but Pinot Noir is perfect for up here."

The Mathewsons replanted the Gewürztraminer and added Riesling, Chardonnay, Pinot Noir and Gamay Noir, thoughtfully selecting grapes varieties able to survive and ripen at 6,470 feet.

Terror Creek's first vintage was 1992 and today their wines still reflect their love for dry, elegant, Alsatian-style wines. Their altitude-friendly Pinot Noir, in particular, is as Burgundian in character as any wine produced outside of France.

"That's how it should be," says Joan, reflecting on the changing tastes of American wine drinkers. "Our European visitors love our wines because they are easy to drink and long lasting."

She said her Pinot Noir will keep 5 to 10 years, "as long as you keep them quiet and the temperature steady."

Is there a secret about making wines at the roof of the world?

"It's a matter of choosing the right grape, a grape that will grow and what you do in the winemaking," Joan explains as she recalls the travails of learning about the unique terroir of Colorado and Garvin Mesa.

"You try to choose the right clone to match the weather and the altitude, but sometimes, no matter what you do …" And her voice trails off to a light laugh.

"It's not always easy, you know?"

West Elk Mountains from Terror Creek Winery

Terror Creek Winery

17445 Garvin Mesa Road, Paonia, CO 81428;
(970) 527-3484;
terrorcreekwinery.com
Est.: 1992 **Owners:** John and Joan Mathewson **Winemaker:** Joan Mathewson **Wines produced:** Chardonnay, Riesling, Gewürztraminer and Pinot Noir **Price range:** $15 to $25 **Annual production:** 800 cases **Tasting room:** Open from 11 a.m. to 5 p.m. Memorial Day to Sept. 30 and weekends only in October. **Other amenities:** Picnic grounds available overlooking the vineyards and West Elk Mountains.

Terror Creek

WEST ELKS

Riesling
·DRY·

PRODUCED AND BOTTLED BY TERROR CREEK WINERY
PAONIA, CO 81428   ALCOHOL 12.9% BY VOLUME   CONTAINS SULFITES

North Fork Valley Wineries

Winemaker's choice: "Our Chardonnay, made in stainless steel, no oak, is extremely flexible and can be enjoyed with almost any food."

Terror Creek is the highest estate winery in the world. There are about 7 acres of Gewürztraminer, Riesling, Chardonnay, Pinot Noir and Gamay Noir grapes growing in mostly clay loam with underlying calcium. Some areas have volcanic rock and gravel, lending a minerality to the white grapes.

"Don't leave our winery without first meeting and making friends with fellow wine lovers, and taking photos to remember well the lovely, beautiful and peaceful mesa-top setting."

Woody Creek Cellars

(Address withheld by request)
Cedaredge, CO 81413; (970) 901-7575;
woodycreekcellars.com
Est.: 2000 **Owner:** Kevin Doyle
Winemaker: Kevin Doyle **Wines
produced:** Cabernet, Merlot, Pinot Noir,
Tempranillo, Sangiovese, Cabernet Franc,
Grenache and Syrah **Price range:** $20 to
$80 **Annual production:** 1,000 cases
Tasting room: 4 p.m. to 10 p.m. Tuesday
through Saturday in Denver at 22nd
& Larimer streets inside the Palma
Cigar Store. Cedaredge by appointment
only. **Tours:** By appointment only.
Other amenities: Picnic grounds with
continental dining. Eclectic art in the
Cedaredge tasting room.
Ask for wine club details

WOODY CREEK CELLARS
LOVE
a warm personal attachment or deep affection
for something or someone

Winemaker's choice: "The Pinot Noir grapes are grown on Cedar Mesa at 6,400 feet and kept for three years in a French oak barrel. This summer drinking wine is best paired with early dinner courses."

Woody Creek Cellars owner and winemaker Kevin Doyle buys all his grapes and pays a little extra, to drop fruit, because the grapes are more intense. Dropping fruit involves thinning grapes later in the season to increase the complexity of the remaining fruit.

The high altitude with cold nights and intense sun produces a smaller, thick-skinned grape with concentrated flavor. He sums up his approach this way: "Treat the vine like a warrior and the wine like a woman."

Woody Creek was awarded 88 points by Harvey Steinman of *Wine Spectator* magazine and awarded several Silver and Bronze medals at the Colorado International Wine Festival.

Doyle makes Old World wine that uses no chemicals and no filters, using gravity flow, and ferments his wines in open bins. His ethos is to make "Handmade wine as they did 1,000 years ago."

*"If I don't grow it, can it, dig it or kill it, I
don't eat it. I am the epitome of slow food."*

**"Don't leave our winery without first calling a friend and asking
them to join you."**

Four Corners Wineries

Cliff Palace at Mesa Verde National Park near Cortez

Four Corners Wineries

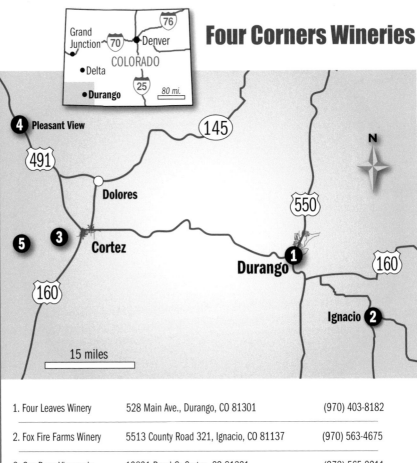

Grand Junction · Denver
COLORADO
· Delta
· Durango
80 mi.

4 Pleasant View

491

145

550

Dolores

5 **3** Cortez

Durango **1**

160

160

Ignacio **2**

N

15 miles

1. Four Leaves Winery	528 Main Ave., Durango, CO 81301	(970) 403-8182
2. Fox Fire Farms Winery	5513 County Road 321, Ignacio, CO 81137	(970) 563-4675
3. Guy Drew Vineyards	19891 Road G, Cortez, CO 81321	(970) 565-9211
4. Pleasant View Vineyards	22970 County Road 10, Pleasant View, CO 81331	(970) 562-4553
5. Sutcliffe Vineyards	12174 Road G, Cortez, CO 81321	(970) 565-0825

Painted Hand Pueblo ruin in the Canyons of the Ancients National Monument northwest of Cortez

New tradition in an ancient land

Maybe it's the enigmatic ruins hiding their secrets under azure skies, the felt-not-heard echo of ancient drums reverberating through narrow slickrock canyons or the old-as-new mystique of making prize-winning wines where centuries ago some of the earliest Americans lived and farmed, but there definitely is something special about the wineries in the Four Corners area.

This is the only spot in the U.S. where four states meet and it's also the only spot in the U.S. where you can enjoy world-class wines in the shade of the sunburnt rock towers at nearby Mesa Verde National Park, where Native Americans strode 600 years before Columbus discovered sailing.

McElmo Canyon, site of the area's two largest wineries (Guy Drew Vineyards and Sutcliffe Vineyards), is a well-watered, narrow valley west of Cortez. The canyon lies within an area replete with mineral-rich clay and sandy loam alluvial soils laid down by an ancient sea and where humans have cultivated life-nourishing crops for 2,000 years.

The southerly region's elevation (5,700 feet above sea level) affords intense sunlit days and cool nights, perfect for maturing grapes with the proper balance of fruit and acidity. The setting also keeps the land free of the vineyard pests and diseases found in other growing areas.

Ancient pottery shards in the Four Corners area

This demanding high-desert environment, where winter freezes, late-spring frosts and pounding summer hail storms all take their toll, asks much from the vines and the winemakers. But the wineries persist, growing both *Vitis vinifera* (Merlot, Cabernet Sauvignon, Cabernet Franc, Syrah, Petit Verdot and Chardonnay, among others) along with some experimental plantings of American hybrids such as the cold-resistant Baco Noir.

This is an irresistible land. In a day's span you might discover a prehistoric rock dwelling peppered with pottery shards from a millennia past and a few hours later enjoy the fruits of modern winemaking with the men and women of the Four Corners region who are forging a new tradition.

Both experiences will bring you back, time and again.

Four Leaves Winery

528 Main Ave., Durango, CO 81301; (970) 403-8182; fourleaveswinery.com; winery@winerymsprings.com
Est.: 2012 **Owners:** Dean and Tracy Fagner **Winemaker:** Dean Fagner **Wines produced:** Green Apple Riesling, Peach Chardonnay, Grapefruit Blush, Cranberry Shiraz, Blackberry Merlot, Black Cherry Pinot Noir, Raspberry Pinot Noir, Viognier, Riesling, Pinot Grigio, Chardonnay, Sangiovese, Pinot Noir, Malbec, Barbera, Tempranillo, Cabernet Sauvignon/Merlot and Zinfandel/Shiraz **Price range:** $15.99 to $19.99; $28.99 for Ports **Annual production:** 3,000 cases
Tasting room: Open noon to 8 p.m. every day. **Tours:** Available upon request. **Other amenities:** Gift shop with wine-related items. Event facilities for 35 seated or 65 mingling. Light appetizers.
Ask for wine club details

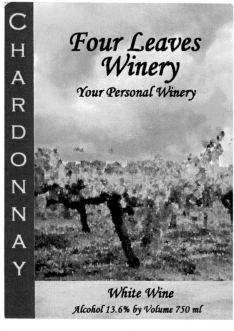

Four Leaves Winery is truly your personal winery.

Located in historic downtown Durango, Four Leaves is a boutique winery and wine bar offering a full range of experiences from wine tastings, to service by the glass, to bottles to go. Four Leaves imports an expansive variety of grapes and fruits and blends and ferments them on site.

Take it a step further and wannabe-winemakers can work with Four Leaves staff to make their own blend, with options limited only by the boundaries of the amateur enologist's imagination. Start with a house wine, then choose oak, tannin, spice and flavor options to suit. Make Your Own Wine is available in batch quantities for 28 bottles of wine, ready in two to four months. You can even create your own custom label.

"We offer the perfect environment to sample and learn about wines."

"Don't leave our winery without first having a picture taken with Maya (the winery dog)."

Fox Fire Farms Winery

5513 County Road 321, Ignacio, CO 81137; (970) 563-4675; foxfirefarms.com; info@foxfirefarms.com

Est.: 2009 **Owners:** Richard and Linda Parry **Winemaker:** Richard Parry **Wines produced:** Riesling, Merlot, Cabernet Sauvignon, Pinot Noir, Chardonnay, Marquette, Corot Noir, Fox Fire Red; fruit wines: Blackberry, Strawberry and Pomegranate **Price range:** $14 to $25 **Annual production:** 500 cases **Tasting room:** Open 1 to 6 p.m. daily May 1 through Oct. 31. Closed in the winter, but tastings can be made by appointment. **Other amenities:** The Villa and winery can host events and weddings for up to 300 people. Picnic grounds are extensive. Appetizers can be provided by appointment.

Fox Fire has a long and storied history of being the Southwest's premier, certified-organic farm.

Arthur and Dovie Jones moved into the Pine River valley east of Ignacio in the early 1900s. They raised sheep, Holstein milk cows and laying hens, while experimenting with beef cattle, pigs and turkeys. Arthur and Dovie also raised two daughters: Alberta and Evelyn. The girls lived the life of the Wild West, taming a cougar and coyotes as pets, and riding horses 2 miles to the one-room country school.

That schoolhouse has been fully restored and can be toured today.

"A sheep is featured on every bottle of wine in honor of our rich history."

Both daughters attended college in the 1930s and became schoolteachers. Alberta married Evan Parry, and Evelyn married Glen Payne.

Five generations of the Jones, Parry and Payne families have lived on the family farm. In the 1970s, the Parry side of the farm was named Fox Fire Farms after the *Foxfire* books, which had started as a student magazine project at an experimental private school in Georgia. Students interviewed local people about their southern Appalachian culture. The articles were turned into books whose folk themes resonated with the back-to-the-land movement of the 1970s.

Foxfire is a term for bioluminescence — emission of light — in fungi in the forests of North Georgia.

Fox Fire Farms is still a functioning sheep and cattle ranch in addition to the more recently added vineyards and winery, and special events hosting.

Visitors can tour the vineyards and 1,100-acre organic livestock farm. There are 6 acres — and growing — of vineyards of Riesling and French American hybrids: Marquette, Traminette, Vignoles, Corot Noir and Noiret.

"Don't leave our winery without first touring our beautiful Colorado setting."

Guy Drew Vineyards: 'We have the land and the winemakers'

Guy Drew kicks the dirt at his feet and a puff of ladybug-red dust rides the breeze toward Utah.

His eyes lance into the distance, ignoring the scatter of ancient ruins abandoned seven centuries ago by the mysterious Ancestral Puebloans.

"This is the future of grape growing in Colorado," he says, sweeping a jacketed arm toward a horizon dominated by the distinctive profile of Sleeping Ute Mountain. "Imagine thousands of acres of premium wine grapes growing as far as you can see. It can be done, I know it."

Guy may have his feet in the ancient past and his heart in the present, but his head is in the future.

The future, for him, is now.

In 1998, Guy and Ruth Drew left their first careers on Colorado's Front Range for the red-rock canyons and juniper-covered mesas of southwest Colorado, dreaming of growing grapes and crafting world-class wines.

Theirs wasn't an Arcadian, get-away-from-it-all quest but instead a desire to develop a winery in the heart of a well-watered canyon surrounded by high-country desert.

Together, they planted the vineyards and built their Guy Drew Vineyards and contemporary Southwest-style home on a 155-acre former hay ranch in McElmo Canyon, one of the rare, year-round streams in this singular part of the country where four states adjoin corners.

The winery and the Drews' spacious straw-bale home lie tucked against the canyon's north wall, connected to the main road across McElmo Creek by a sturdy bridge spanning a ragged gully torn from the earth during the 1911 flood that ripped through the canyon, sweeping entire hayfields and apple orchards into Utah.

Guy's initial vintages of 2000–2003 were labeled Crooked Creek because his own vines weren't yet mature and he initially used grapes grown in the Grand Valley and later in vineyards in McElmo Canyon.

Since then, however, using grapes he raises on his farm along with those he purchases from Colorado's best

Guy Drew Vineyards
west of Cortez

growers, Guy Drew Vineyards has filled out to include a 1,400-square-foot crush.

That Guy has succeeded in his quest for world-class wines is unquestioned, both by his many fans and the enthusiastic reception his wines have received from such well-known wine literati as the ebullient Gary Vaynerchuk of "Wine Library TV."

"He gave us a triple 'Wow,'" chuckles Guy as he recalls Vaynerchuk's unexpected gusto in his initial tasting of Guy Drew wines and Colorado wines in general.

Guy Drew wines also have been lauded in *Sunset* magazine and *The Washington Post*. Joe Roberts of 1winedude.com and *Playboy* magazine termed Guy Drew's 2011 Pinot Gris one of "10 best" wines tasted that year.

But Guy is restless and sees yet more possibilities for his region's winemaking.

Which is why he stands sentinel-like in an unplowed field under a dome of unblemished Persian-blue sky.

Already he has produced a tiny bottling of premium wine from a pocket-sized vineyard grown nearby, but it's not what you might expect.

This particular wine was dry-farmed, relying like the ancients on nature to supply the irrigation, and is made from Baco Noir, an unsung hybrid grape presently little-grown in Colorado. Known for its cold-resistant qualities, Baco Noir can be lush, dry and infused with blueberry and plum.

Most Colorado wines are made from the familiar European vinifera grape varieties, but those grapes are susceptible to Colorado's cold winters and seasonal frosts.

Guy sees the future as one blending hybrids and vinifera, a future rooted in the Four Corners region where the rich red fields roll wave-like into the distance.

"This is the only place in Colorado where we have enough acreage to produce enough grapes to support a large winery," he says to a rising wind. "We have the land and the winemakers, now we need the grapes."

Guy Drew Vineyards sits on 155 acres on McElmo Creek west of Cortez

Guy Drew Vineyards

19891 Road G, Cortez, CO 81321;
(970) 565-9211; guydrewvineyards.com;
guydrew@q.com

Est.: 1999 **Owners:** Guy and Ruth Drew **Winemaker:** Guy Drew **Wines produced:** Unoaked Chardonnay, Pinot Gris, Viognier, Riesling from dry to sweet, Merlot, Cabernet Sauvignon, Syrah, Bordeaux blends, sweet red, and white and red dessert wines **Price range:** $16 to $30 **Annual production:** 3,500 cases **Tasting room:** Open every day from noon to 5 p.m. There is also a seasonal tasting room at 27601 E. Highway 160, on the east side of Cortez at Mesa Indian Trading Company and Gallery. Hours are 1 to 6 p.m. May through mid-October. **Tours:** Offered rarely and by appointment only. **Other amenities:** Bistro tables for bring-your-own picnic. Small events may be hosted by appointment.
Ask for wine club details

Winemaker's choice: "A red blend we call Metate, not always available, pairs well with hearty beef or lamb dishes."

Guy Drew Vineyards' wines have been praised by nationally known critics such as Gary Vaynerchuk of "Wine Library" fame. Joe Roberts of 1winedude blog and *Playboy* magazine called the 2011 Pinot Gris one of his Top Ten "most interesting" wines he tasted in 2012. Guy Drew wines also have been featured in *Sunset* magazine, *The Washington Post*, *Westword*, *The Denver Post*, *The Aspen Times*, *The Grand Junction Daily Sentinel*, *The Colorado Springs Gazette* and hometown papers *The Durango Herald* and the *Cortez Journal*.

Six acres of estate vineyards are being replanted to lesser-known varieties such as Norton/Cynthiana, Baco Noir and Marquette, to suit the micro-climate.

"My favorite proverb is 'People who love what they do never work another day in their life.'"

"Don't leave our winery without first taking a big breath of fresh air, drink a glass of wine and enjoy the beauty of McElmo Canyon."

Pleasant View Vineyards

22970 County Road 10,
Pleasant View, CO 81331;
(970) 562-4553;
pleasantviewvineyards.info;
pvvineyards@fone.net
Est.: 2001 **Owners and winemakers:**
Allan and Elizabeth Bleak **Wines
produced:** Chardonnay and Pinot
Noir **Price range:** $28 to $30 **Annual
production:** 1,000 cases
No tasting room

Pleasant View Vineyards is only open
to the public during the annual harvest
party; email for an invitation. Wine
can be tasted and purchased at the
Pleasant View Mercantile's Farmers
Market 4 to 8 p.m. Wednesdays from
June 1 through Oct. 31.

*"We believe
in quality, not
quantity. We have
our hands in every
aspect of our
wine process from
growing the grapes
and managing the
vineyard to the
finished bottled
product."*

Pleasant View Vineyards is one of the highest vineyards
in the world at 6,912 feet of high-desert elevation. That
makes for risky growing, but fantastic wine. The hot, sunny
days that make Colorado summers a pleasure also mature
the fruit and build its natural sugars. The chill that gives
the nights their crisp bite has a similar effect on the wine,
helping the grapes retain the acids that vintners prize.
The landscape and climate give these wines a distinctive
Colorado canyon country character.

Allan and Elizabeth Bleak in 2001 cleared old-growth
forest to plant their vineyard. Through trial and error they
established a 10-acre organic orchard and vineyard,
growing Chardonnay, Pinot Noir, Merlot, Cabernet
Sauvignon and Pinot Blanc. They've been propagating their
own vines since 2007 with great success and are naturalist
winemakers. They rely solely on the grape and its seasonal
differences without the use of sulfites, enzymes, additives
or sugar. Fermentation naturally happens, and the wine's aging and mellowing comes
from resting within sustainable, untreated, French oak barrels.

Pleasant View's 2009 Chardonnay was awarded The American Wine Society 2012
Governor's Cup Bronze Medal. The 2010 Chardonnay in 2013 was awarded the Beverage
Testing Institute World Value Wine Challenge Bronze Medal.

**"Don't leave our winery without first experiencing the annual
harvest party and processing of the grapes."**

Sutcliffe Vineyards: We're 'immensely proud of our authenticity'

Next to a sharp bend in McElmo Creek where it curls beneath a bull-nosed sandstone monolith called Battle Rock, John Sutcliffe is perpetuating history with his wines.

His eponymous Sutcliffe Vineyards is forging a modern tack on the 2,000-year-old narrative of farming along the banks of the creek, once the homeland of the Ancestral Puebloans, the mysterious, cliff-dwelling forebears of today's Pueblo cultures of the Rio Grande Valley and elsewhere in the Southwest.

How did a former British military officer-turned-restaurateur (including New York City's famed Tavern on the Green)–turned Colorado cowboy end up in this ravine-cleft corner of Colorado where the crystalline air is shattered by a raven's harsh croak?

John, a Welshman whose first love might well be the polo field, delights in telling the story of how he purchased the 200-acre ranch in 1990 while driving home from a vacation with his now ex-wife Emily to Canyonlands National Park in southeast Utah.

As the story goes, they were taking the narrow road through McElmo Canyon toward Cortez when a hand-scripted sign changed their lives.

"She was driving and there was this sign along the side of the road that said, 'Peaches, tomatoes, melons, ranch,'" he says, laughing heartily. "We came in and bought all four."

John talks and thinks in legato, the words and visions braided as tightly as the cordage occasionally discovered hidden in the countless ruins dotting the landscape.

Because of the winery's distance from major population centers, John decided that instead of relying on a tasting room to market his wines, he would draw on his background in the posh restaurant business to get his wines in front of the clientele he desired.

"When we started making wines here (his first vintage was 1997), I think we came out of the box," he says, his words clipped and clean. "We concentrate on really good, high-end

Sutcliffe Vineyards is 12 miles west of Cortez

restaurants because I built 20 of them myself and that's what I know."

John's vineyard and winery is 12 miles west of Cortez on Montezuma County Road G, more often called the McElmo Canyon Road and what locals sometimes call, tongue firmly in cheek, the Cortez-to-Bluff (Utah) "highway."

"We're a bit isolated here, which means our visitors really want to come here, and I make it worth their while," John offers cheerily.

Although he occasionally hosts guests at the winery, he's opening a formal tasting room in Durango, about 57 miles from the front door of his self-designed Spanish-style house.

His wines have earned national attention from such renowned wine publications as *Wine Spectator* and *Wine Enthusiast*, while his two-story home

Sutcliffe Vineyards' first vintage was 1997

and four-level guest house have been featured prominently in several slick-cover, town-and-country-type magazines.

His website offers 20 wines, including a couple with names rooted to John's youth in Wales: Ael y Bryn ("top of the hill"), a Rhone-style blend of Syrah, Grenache and Cinsault; and Trawsfynydd ("across the mountain"), a Bordeaux-style blend of Cabernet Franc, Merlot, Petit Verdot and Cabernet Sauvignon.

After making his first namesake vintage in 1995, John has deferred the winemaking to the talents of others.

"At first, I was making the wines and then in 2003 Ben (Parsons) came on," says John. "After Ben left (to create his Infinite Monkey Theorem label), I lured Joe Buckel away from Flowers in 2008. He is a bloody genius, what I call the Charles Dickens of winemaking. His methods are absolutely traditional and he has immense respect for the grapes and for the farming we do."

Max Ariza, a sommelier and wine instructor at Johnson and Wales University in Denver, has called Sutcliffe Vineyards' wines among "the upper tier" of the state's wines and said the McElmo Canyon juice can "compete with any wine in the U.S."

John can't hide his pleasure.

"I let my wines speak for themselves. We are immensely proud of our authenticity."

Sutcliffe Vineyards

12174 Road G, Cortez, CO 81321;
(970) 565-0825; sutcliffewines.com;
info@sutcliffewines.com
Est.: 1995 **Owner:** John Sutcliffe
Winemaker: Joe Buckel **Wines produced:**
Chardonnay, Merlot, Petit Verdot, Syrah
and Cabernet Sauvignon **Price range:** $20
to $40 **Annual production:** 4,000 cases
Tasting room: Open every day from 10
a.m. to 5 p.m. **Tours:** Available year-round.
Other amenities: Patio with bistro tables.
Catering by Dunton Hot Springs with advance
arrangements.
Ask for wine club details

Winemaker's choice: "Chardonnay Signature
from Castillo Vineyard paired with chicken."

Merlot and Chardonnay grapes are raised
on a 7-acre vineyard next to the winery.
Other vineyards in McElmo Canyon grow
Cabernet Sauvignon, Syrah and Petit Verdot
for Sutcliffe. Terroir includes a very subtle
peanut brittle smell and taste in the red
wines specific to the canyon.

"We farm our wines organically. We also produce and sell hay and
seasonal vegetables and host many events such as a Harvest Dinner,
which can be found on our website."

"Don't leave our winery without first trying the Doce Pecado (our
Port) or talking to John Sutcliffe."

By AMY NUERNBERG

"Wine from Colorado?" people gasp as they envision extreme red rocks or Rocky Mountains. Isn't Colorado better known for powder snow and glitzy historic mining towns?

It's an unlikely landscape at an altitude of 4,500 to 6,400 feet, with a short growing season, wild temperature variations and barely 10 inches of rainfall. But the story of today's vibrant wine scene started in the desert scrub cut by the Colorado River in Western Colorado.

Visionaries, entrepreneurs, dreamers, farmers, legislators, money, national events, weather — and that magic in a bottle — all play a part in the drama.

Amy Nuernberg christens a vineyard

First the grapes

Imagine the 1880s. Land developers eyed dusty flats around Palisade as potential farms if the land could be irrigated with the Colorado River. Canals were built and parcels sold. Predictions that peaches and grapes could be grown profitably lured European immigrants with winemaking traditions. Notables like Grand Junction founder George Crawford also planted grapes.

Interest grew in foreign wine grapes, *Vitis vinifera,* over native American table grapes, *Vitis lambrusca.* In 1909 a U.S. Department of Agriculture report stated that over a million pounds of grapes was harvested in Colorado.

Meanwhile, a temperance movement was fermenting, and the 18th Amendment prohibited alcohol sales in 1919. Severe winters furthered the demise of vines as Palisade growers replanted with fruit trees.

Early agriculture in Palisade

Prohibition ended in 1933 during the Depression. It took the affluent 1950s to rekindle the allure of wine, influenced by travel abroad and on TV, Julia Child's French cooking show.

Then the wine

Colorado's first modern winery, Ivancie Cellars, opened in Denver in 1968. From a Slavic winemaking tradition, Dr. Gerald Ivancie made premium wines and hired consultant Warren Winiarski (founder of Napa's Stag's Leap Winery). The wines won international awards and favorable press. Gerald and wife Mary hosted classy wine parties attended by trendsetters at their Cherry Creek mansion.

Winiarski sourced California grapes, but the cost tripled in six years. Seeing the future depended on local grapes, Ivancie funded experimental plantings with six Palisade

IVANCIE CELLARS
AMERICAN
Cabernet Sauvignon
1968
PRODUCED AND BOTTLED BY IVANCIE WINES, INC.,
DENVER, COLORADO BW3
ALCOHOL 13% BY VOLUME

Gerald and Mary Ivancie

peach farmers who were keen to diversify after a series of freezes. Things did not go well: First the vines withered, then Ivancie Cellars closed in 1975.

An industry flourishes

Pioneer growers got help with research funding from the Four Corners Regional Commission. Their 1981 report examined Colorado, Arizona, Utah and New Mexico, identifying the optimal combination of soils, climates and grape varieties to produce fine wine. Colorado State University's agricultural research stations received a grant to continue the study locally.

Ripples from Ivancie Cellars spread. Jim and Ann Seewald owned winemaking supply shops in Denver. In 1978, with investors, some Ivancie equipment and Palisade acreage, Colorado Mountain Vineyards established the first farm winery, then moved to a Palisade vineyard in 1981. The Seewalds promoted Colorado wine and helped establish a trade group and the federal designation of the Grand Valley as

a winegrowing region. Colorado Mountain Vineyards won top medals, but closed.

New owners renamed it Colorado Cellars.

Commitment to the future

The Seewalds inspired others. Bennett and Davy Price started a vineyard-planting and supply business (launching DeBeque Canyon Winery in 1997). Plum Creek Cellars, now known as Plum Creek Winery, opened in Larkspur in 1984 and moved to Palisade in 1989. Parker and Mary Carlson began Carlson Vineyards in 1988. Stephen Smith acquired land during the 1980s energy bust era for a vineyard operation, and Grande River Vineyards

Ann Seewald at Colorado Mountain Vineyards in 1982

planted grapes in 1987.

Seeking support to grow the new wine business, the fledging wineries recruited Western Colorado legislators. An act was passed in 1990, creating a board to direct grape-growing and winemaking research, market Colorado wines and promote tourism. Funding came from a penny a liter tax on all wine sold in Colorado.

Since then, more than 100 wineries have sprung up statewide, yet Palisade's unique terroir remains the source of most grapes. In 2009 the Mesa Land Trust began its "Fruitlands Forever" initiative to conserve 1,000 acres of vineyards and orchards. The goal is to preserve their economic value and ensure the sustainability of fruit growing in Palisade for future generations.

■

My gratitude to those who engaged in making Colorado wine what it is today, and shared their time, expertise and stories with me for this book: Stephen Smith, Sue Phillips, Parker and Mary Carlson, Dr. Gerald Ivancie, Liz Ivancie Kennedy, John Lowey, Debbie Kovalik, Tilman Bishop, Colorado Wine Industry Development Board, Cassidee Shull, Kelli Hepler, Priscilla Walker, Michael Menard and Judy Prosser-Armstrong. Thank you Jay Seaton and Laurena Mayne Davis for the invitation to contribute to this project.

Mary and Parker Carlson of Carlson Vineyards

Overview of Colorado Mountain Vineyards in 1982

How to taste wine

By SUE PHILLIPS
Owner Plum Creek Winery
By JENNE BALDWIN-EATON
Winemaker for Plum Creek
Winery

Going to a winery to taste wines is much like arriving at someone's home. You can be assured of friendly folks wanting to greet visitors upon arrival. Don't feel intimidated walking into a winery even if you are new to tasting wines. The goal of a winery is to create a comfortable ambiance, meeting old friends and making new ones.

Wherever you go in Western Colorado you will find a lot of enthusiasm for the art of making wine and educating people about wine quality. Most tasting rooms have a selection of wine-themed and unusual gifts, so feel free to browse before or after your tasting.

Sue Phillips and Jenne Baldwin-Eaton with Plum Creek Winery

Once you arrive at the tasting bar, expect to produce identification showing you are at least 21. This is something that protects everyone involved to ensure compliance with the liquor laws of the state of Colorado. Once that is over with, get ready to enjoy wine.

There is no set time for a wine tasting. How long you want to linger is up to you. Sometimes serendipity strikes and your visit coincides with other winemaking tasks, such as bottling. Most wineries don't mind if you have a peek to see how the winemaking magic comes together with a glass bottle, label, capsule and cork. If you want to visit other wineries, however, you will want to keep an eye on your watch because time can slip by quickly when you are enjoying tasty Colorado wines.

Once the tasting begins, most wineries have a recommended order for tasting, but this is never a hard-and-fast rule, so feel free to skip ahead to a different wine you know you will like. Policies vary, so you will find that some wineries charge a tasting fee, others do not.

It is an easy step-by-step process for tasting wine. After the taste is poured, hold up your glass to examine the color and clarity of the wine. Next, swirl the glass to activate the esters, or flavor compounds, of the wine. Put your nose into the glass

91

and breathe in the complex scents to figure out what smells you detect. In a well-made Sauvignon Blanc there may be citrus and fig, with a herbaceous quality. In a Cabernet Sauvignon you may smell raspberry, leather and oak. And then you get to the best part — take a taste.

Part of the fun at a tasting room is trying new wines. Even if you don't think you will like a particular wine, give it a try and experiment with something new. You may discover a wine you never knew you would enjoy. Still, if you are certain you do not want to try something, it is appropriate to let the tasting room staff know. No offense is taken, and it will save from consigning an otherwise good wine to the dump bucket.

Most tastings are self-paced. Look to the winery staffer to guide you through the wines. Most employees are quite knowledgeable about the winemaking style of each wine, the wine statistics, source of where the grapes were grown and recommended pairings with food. Feel free to ask questions. Winemakers love seeing people's enthusiasm for the wines, and they often will spend more time one-on-one with tasting room visitors. In the winery business it is the personal connection with people that is so satisfying.

There is one simple rule of etiquette: If you were invited to dinner at a neighbor's home, would you, upon tasting the food, remark loudly to everyone there, "This is awful! I

Two Rivers Winery

hate this!" Of course not.

The same is true at a tasting room. If you dislike a particular wine, simply pour the taste into the dump bucket. Save critical comments, if they must be said, for the time after you leave the winery.

Finally, have fun and enjoy the tasting room experience.

Parker Carlson of Carlson Vineyards

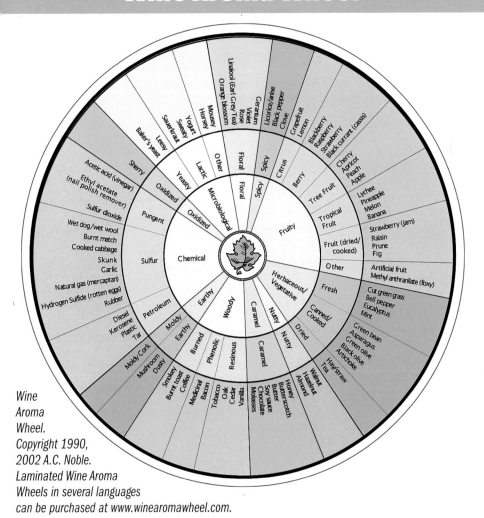

Wine
Aroma
Wheel.
Copyright 1990,
2002 A.C. Noble.
Laminated Wine Aroma
Wheels in several languages
can be purchased at www.winearomawheel.com.

The easy-to-use Wine Aroma Wheel works from the inside out to help wine tasters articulate increasingly specific aromas when tasting wine.

Widely adopted, the wheel was invented in 1984 by Professor Ann C. Noble at the University of California, Davis, as a way to encourage a common language in wine tasting and help novice wine tasters develop their proficiency.

The wheel has general terms located in the center, such as "fruity," radiating out to the most specific terms in the outer tier, such as "blackberry." Easy to use and understand, it can enhance your whole wine experience.

Wine pronunciation guide

Wine names are an international melting pot. Because they're often derived from the region in which the grapes traditionally had been grown, they can be real tongue-twisters of French, German, Italian and Spanish origin.

Don't let a name keep you from trying a wine. Everyone stumbles over a Gewürztraminer (geh VERTZ trah mee ner) from time to time. And, really. Do you want to go through life ordering nothing but a "red." There's more out there to explore!

Below is a pronunciation guide to many of the wines of Western Colorado. And if that doesn't work, point to the label and ask your friendly tasting room pourer, "How do you pronounce that?"

Baco Noir \ BAH ko NWAR
Barbera \ bar BEH rah
Burgundy \ BUR gun dee
Cabernet Franc \ cab er NAY franhk
Cabernet Sauvignon \ cab er NAY saw veen YON
Chablis \ sha BLEE
Chambourcin \ shom boor sahn
Chardonnay \ shar dun NAY
Gamay Noir \ GAM may nwahr
Gewürztraminer \ geh VERTZ trah mee ner
Grenache \ greh NOSH
Le Crescent \ leh CRES ent
Lemberger \ LEM ber ger
Malbec \ Mall beck
Merlot \ mer LOW
Muscadet \ MOOS cah day
Muscat \ moos CAHT
Petite Syrah \ peh TEET sih-RAH
Pinot Blanc \ PEE-noh BLAHN
Pinot Grigio \ pee no GREE jho
Pinot Gris \ pee no GREE
Pinot Noir \ pee no NWAHR
Riesling \ REES ling
Rkatsiteli \ Reh KATS eh tellie
Rosé \ roe ZAY
Sangiovese \ san joe VA say
Sauvignon Blanc \ saw veen YON blan
Sémillon \ say mee YOHN
Syrah \ sih RAH
Tempranillo \ tem pra NEE oh
Viognier \ vee oh NYAY
Zinfandel \ ZIN fun dell

Vino vocabulary

Aging. The ability of a wine to improve as it gets older. Generally more true for red wines than white wines and influenced by many factors, including grape variety, storage techniques and winemaking style.

American Viticultural Area. A designated geographic wine area having certain distinctive characteristics for growing grapes. Colorado has two, both in Western Colorado: Grand Valley and West Elks.

Appellation. A legally defined and protected geographic area indicating where wine grapes are grown (see AVA).

Balanced. The notion a wine is balanced when its tannins, fruit and acidity are in harmony.

Jay Christianson, co-owner of Canyon Wind Cellars

Body. The feel or weight of the wine in the mouth. Consider the differences between skim milk, whole milk and heavy cream.

CAVE. Acronym for Colorado Association for Viticulture and Enology. This member-based organization based in Palisade, Colo., supports winemaking and viticulture in the state.

Colorado Wine Industry Development Board. This governor-appointed board promotes and markets winemaking in the state under the authority of the Colorado Department of Agriculture.

Enology. (ee-nol-uh-gee) The science and study of wine and winemaking.

Finish. The flavors lingering in the mouth after having swallowed or spat a wine.

Fortified. Wines with brandy or other spirits added, such as Port or Sherry.

Ice Wine. (Eiswein in Germany) A sweet, dessert-style wine made from grapes frozen on the vine. Most come from Germany and Canada.

Magnum. A 1.5-liter bottle that's twice as big as regular bottles. Even bigger: Nebuchadnezzar, which is 15 liters or the equivalent of 20 regular bottles.

Meritage. (rhymes with "heritage") A branded trademark for Bordeaux-style blended red and white wines.

New World Wines. Wines made outside the traditional winegrowing countries of Europe. Also refers to a style of wine, which often is riper, higher in alcohol and more fruit-forward.

Oak. Wood used in winemaking to add complexity and various flavors to wines. Most often oak barrels are used during fermentation and aging, but they're also used in other methods, such as chips, staves and oak additives.

95

Old World Wines. Wines originating in Europe and parts of the Mediterranean Basin where tradition and terroir are dominant. Often lower in alcohol, less fruity and considered more elegant.

Reserve wines. A term that implies higher quality or something special but is often more a marketing term than an indicator of quality.

Sediment. Naturally occurring, harmless residue found in some bottles, especially older and unfiltered wines.

Sommelier. (som-all-yay) A trained wine professional who has completed courses of study in all aspects of wine service.

Stainless Steel. Wines said to be "all stainless steel" were fermented in temperature-controlled steel tanks and meant to be fresh, fruity and aromatic.

Sulfites. Naturally occurring substance also used to preserve and stabilize wines. Present in virtually all wines. Often incorrectly blamed for headaches.

Tannins. Naturally occurring substances that give red wines their backbone and contribute to their longevity. They make a wine taste dry.

Terroir. Refers to the specificity of place or the "whereness" from which a wine originates. Also, the natural conditions in a particular locale that determine the characteristics in wine from that place.

Varietal. A wine named for a grape type, such as Chardonnay. In the United States, a wine must be at least 75% of a grape type to be labeled a varietal.

Vinifera. (or *Vitis vinifera*) Species of vine that produces classic European wine grapes such as Cabernet Sauvignon and most of the commercial wines produced today.

Vintage. The year grapes were harvested.

Viticulture. The process of growing grapes.

Wine club. A program offered by many wineries that allows members to receive discounted wine purchases periodically through the year.

Yeast. Naturally occurring organism that causes fermentation, the conversion of sugar into alcohol. Winemakers often add custom yeast strains to promote fermentation and achieve certain flavors in wine.

Straight from the barrel at Plum Creek Winery

11-08.

Growing grapes in Western Colorado

The story of grape growing in Western Colorado is as tangled as the vines knotting themselves around old fenceposts and wire trellises.

And no less diverse than the multitude of nationalities and cultures that settled here is the diversity of grapes you discover in shadowed neighborhoods and planted in deliberate, leafy rows.

From that early cultivation by pioneers such as Grand Junction founder George Crawford and by Italian, Slovenian and other immigrants, grape growers unfamiliar with the climatic fortunes of Western Colorado planted what they were familiar with and what they liked to eat or drink.

Unsurprisingly, today's winemakers are no different.

While some of those first plantings were the familiar European *Vitis vinifera* varieties popular with wine drinkers, there also were many grapes — both white and red — more familiar to the homemaker than the winemaker.

During the gloomy days of Prohibition home winemaking took on a new relevance, but it wasn't until 1968, 35 years after the repeal of Prohibition, when Denver periodontist Gerald Ivancie opened Colorado's first post-Prohibition winery, that Colorado's grape industry turned its face toward wine.

Initially Ivancie sourced grapes from California, but as those prices rose, engendered by short crops and increased demand, by early 1973 he was contracting with farmers in the Grand Valley — a 40-mile-long swath of river bottom through the heart of Mesa County — to grow wine grapes from cuttings imported from California.

The initial efforts failed when the cuttings did not survive their first winter, and by the time the second generation was in the ground, Ivancie was out of the wine business.

Also in 1973, the Four Corners Regional Commission began investigating the economics of grape growing in Colorado, Utah, Arizona and New Mexico, an offshoot of which is the Colorado State University

State viticulturist
Horst Caspari

Orchard Mesa Research Station, which has been a boon to grape growers across Western Colorado.

A small handful of those Four Corners project plots still exist and produce grapes today, but most of them failed due to lack of attention or simply because the methods followed were those from California wine country, which has neither Colorado's high elevations nor its gelid winters.

But growers also discovered the positive aspects of high-altitude grape cultivation: The intense sunlight and cooler, longer growing seasons promote the complex chemical components (phenols) that add intense color and vibrant aromas to wine.

Plus, broad diurnal temperature swings, sometimes 50 degrees or more difference between day and night, promote the food-friendly acidity characteristic of Colorado wine.

Richard A. Hamman Jr., the first viticulturist at the Orchard Mesa Research Station, initiated early experimenting with grape varieties — planting them, cultivating them and hanging them on wires — and as he learned he shared that knowledge with experienced and would-be winemakers.

What Richard learned, and his successor, current state viticulturist Horst Caspari still preaches, is that some grapes handle Colorado better than others.

That divination, the reading of the runes formed by those gnarled vines braided across miles of wires and cordon systems, is guiding the future of Colorado grape growing.

"The demand for grapes continues to grow," says Horst. "That means more pressure on the vineyards to produce, but we are rapidly running out of the best places to grow vinifera grapes, if we haven't already."

It's also learning to deal with what winemaker Kenn Dunn of Hermosa Vineyards calls Colorado's "three winters": early winter, mid-winter and late winter.

Some grape varietals are hit hardest by early winter cold snaps, some succumb to grim mid-winter cold, and others are knocked down by late-spring frosts.

"Every vintage brings new challenges," Horst says. "The key to great winemaking is knowing what this year's challenge is and recognizing the challenge before it becomes a problem in the winery. Besides, if every vintage were the same, winemaking would be too easy."

While current planting still trends to European *Vitis vinifera* grapes, some adventurous grape growers, seeking vines that might survive all three of Colorado's winters, are turning more and more to disease-resistant and cold-hardy hybrids.

In 2012, Merlot (18 percent of all grapes cultivated in Colorado) continued its long record as the most-popular grape, reflecting how well that particular varietal does in the Grand Valley, which produces about 85 percent of Colorado's wine grapes.

Well behind Merlot in production amount comes Riesling (11.3 percent), Cabernet Sauvignon (10.7), Cabernet Franc (7.4) and Chardonnay (6.8).

Other leading varietals included Syrah (6.7), Gewürztraminer (6.3), Viognier (4) and Pinot Noir (3.6).

Collectively, "others" amounted to more than 25 percent of the grapes grown in Colorado. These may be the grapes you see growing in backyards and test plots and hanging off cedar-post fences. This category includes (but is not limited to) the following (how many can you recognize?):

Carmenere, Carmine, Catawba, Cayuga White, Chambourcin, Chancellor, Chardonel, Chenin Blanc, Concord, Corot Noir, Counoise, Cynthiana (Baco Noir), Dolcetto, Edelweiss, Esprit, Fredonia, French Columbard, Frontenac, Frontenac Gris, Gamay Noir, Graciano, Grenache, Himrod, Isabella, La Crescent, La Crosse, Lemberger, Leon Millot, Malbec, Marechal Foch, Marquette, Montepulciano, Mourvedre, Muscat Blanc, Muscat Hamburg, Muscat Ottonel, Nebbiolo, Noiret, Norton, Orange Muscat, Petit Verdot, Petite Syrah, Pinot Blanc, Pinot Meunier, Primitivo, Rkatsiteli, Rousanne, Sangiovese, Sauvignon Blanc, Semillon, Seyval Blanc, Souzao, St. Croix, St. Laurent, St. Pepin, Tannat, Tempranillo, Tinto Cao, Tinta Madeira, Touriga Nacional, Traminette, Vernaccia, Vidal, Vignoles, Zinfandel and Zweigelt.

The farming life

Lee Bradley, co-owner of Black Bridge Winery near Paonia

By LEE BRADLEY
Black Bridge Winery co-owner

Originally our high-country Paonia farm was home to acres of apples, but the market has changed, and apples are no longer as profitable as other crops.

In 1998, after replacing apples with peaches and sweet cherries, I decided to experiment by planting a small block of Merlot grapes. The wine grapes thrived, so the viticulture adventure continued, and in 2000 I planted Pinot Noir. I found myself hooked on wine grapes and hoped the climate also would be kind to Chardonnay and Riesling grapes.

Viticulture — like all farming — is both science and art. It takes year-round devotion to the land to coax vines from dry soil and through killing frosts.

Life in the vineyards revolves around the weather and the calendar.

In March it's time to prepare the soil for the garden, mark the ground for any new trees or vines, mend fence and clean sprinklers.

April, May and early June are the tricky months. Dependent on Mother Nature and Lady Luck, a fruit farmer hopes there won't be a killing frost. I monitor weather reports and, depending on the stage of bloom, determine what the critical temperature is in order to protect the crop.

I set the wind machine to that fruit-saving temperature, go to bed and try to get some sleep, more likely to wake up and head to the orchards to check the situation.

April and May are for pruning fruit trees and grapevines. This needs to be done whether there is a crop or not. The peaches, pears and cherries need dormant oil applied before bloom. It's also the time to get the irrigation system working, all the while wondering if there is enough snowpack in the mountains to have irrigation water in August and September to ripen all the fruit and grapes.

It's important to have a replant schedule for different blocks of fruit trees. Their life span is about 25 years for quality fruit.

In spring the white wines from the previous year are bottled. This is a temperamental time for white wine, so I keep a watchful eye, at the same time checking to see if the red wines have finished malolactic fermentation, and finding a nice day to move barrels to the cellar for aging. The reds will age for 16 months before they are bottled.

Hopefully there is a bountiful peach crop that requires thinning. This procedure will ensure the remaining peaches are big enough to make a good showing at the packing shed, then on to the grocery stores across the state. Just as fruit trees need to be thinned, vines have to be shoot-thinned and suckered. This will allow grapes to ripen properly.

By the first of June I generally know if the fruit trees and grapevines are going to bear fruit.

It's time to start harvesting cherries in July. This is not the time for a hard rain, which can split ripe cherries and ruin the crop. If cherries survive frost in the spring, and heavy rain and hail at harvest time, I will need to hire just about anyone who can give a good day's work. There is a short window of time to pick cherries before they become overripe. When cherries are done, my wife, Kathy, and I like to sneak in a weekend fishing trip to the mountains where we gather ourselves before peaches start.

Harvesting peaches for the packing shed begins in early August. Varieties of peaches ripen at different times. The crew and I pick for about 25 to 30 days as each variety ripens.

You-pick peaches are the ones left on trees after the picking crew has finished. As these peaches become tree ripe, people show up in droves to get that perfect peach. It doesn't take many of these North Fork beauties to convince people you are the best farmer in the valley.

In September the aged red wine is bottled to make room in the aging barrels for the upcoming grape harvest. All vines must be covered with bird netting to protect them from ravens, sparrows and starlings. These pesky birds can take the crop before it's ready to harvest.

With bins washed, the destemmer and press ready, and hopefully labor enough to begin picking, I wait for the sugar, PH and

Lee Bradley, co-owner of Black Bridge Winery

acid to be just right. Grapes are processed as they're brought in from the vineyards. After destemming, the reds are fermented in bins, and wine is pumped into the aging barrels.

White grapes are pressed and the juice goes into stainless steel tanks for fermentation.

After grape harvest, most of the seasonal migrant labor has gone home for the winter. The retail market is still going strong, and with the onset of fall, wine, you-pick apples, pumpkins and gourds become the hot items.

Rain is a welcome sight after harvest. This moisture will help grapevines survive the sometimes harsh and dry winter. And of course deer and elk are always looking for a free lunch during those late fall and winter months.

Our market closes on Halloween and things settle down. Kathy and I look forward to a little R&R and even get away for a couple of weeks during winter months. It's really hard to tell where one year stops and the next begins, and it's hard to stop farming because there is always something that needs to be done.

After a short winter break, March is upon us, and it's time to begin pruning fruit trees. It's a waiting game to see if the grapevines made it through the winter.

The science of wine

Stephen Menke, Ph.D, state enologist

By STEPHEN MENKE, Ph.D
State enologist

The relationship among grapes, wine and humans comprises the world's most legendary horticultural history. The grape is the world's most valuable horticultural crop. The genetics of the grape make it one of the most responsive of plants to both subtle environmental pressures and horticultural manipulation. This has enabled it to spread widely from its reputed origin in the very singular climate and geography of the south central part of the Gondwanaland supercontinent, now the TransCaucasus, with of course a lot of later help from human caretakers.

But the grape, while tasty, has none of the social power of its yeasty product: wine. Though mood-altering alkaloids in many plants were known to ancient cultures, only alcohol from yeast fermentation was a drug that could alter moods and minds and yet be trusted to have those effects gradually and by volume of intake. Thus alcohol has been the social lubricant of choice for millennia, in the form of wine and beer.

Wine historically has had a much subtler and more diverse sensory impact on humans than beer as well as higher alcohol content from the sweeter grape, making it the choice of alcoholic intoxicants used by shamans and priests to help in altering human relationships via religious ceremonies.

Growing grapes and making wine firstly involves understanding the basic biological

Growing grapes and making wine firstly involves understanding the basic biological science of the grapevine and the yeast organism.

science of the grapevine and the yeast organism. Secondly, it involves the artistry of horticultural and winemaking visualization and manipulation to not only express the genetics of the grape and sensory powers of wine, but to then tie each wine to the longstanding and legendary social history of wine and its creators. And as with all art, innovation by rebellion is a central tenet, which is very evident in our Colorado wine landscape.

Colorado is physically imposing for winegrape horticulture, due to unpredictable cold events, short growing seasons and high altitude dynamics. Colorado is also not a traditional part of wine cultural history, and selling both the idea of and the bottle of wine is as difficult as crossing the central Rockies in a snowstorm. Thus, raising grapes and making wine in Colorado is both a leap of faith and a defiant act of culture. This means that the Western U.S. tradition of self-reliance and rebellion against outside interference is fully exhibited in the Colorado grape and wine industry. Every Colorado grower and winemaker is sure that he or she is the one who will conquer all of the physical and social impediments and make and be recognized for the next great American wine and its successful marketing.

With all of the above being believed, what is the reality and future of Colorado wine? The grape reality is that the traditional *Vitis vinifera* grapes can be grown, with cold event caveats, in the least harsh environments of Colorado. The current generation of accomplished Colorado winemakers is making some excellent wines. These wines often have distinct Colorado terroir and have carved out a place for the Colorado wine brand in the marketplace. The other reality is that these environments are almost fully exploited in Colorado. This means that the wine industry will remain small, unless either grapes are imported from better climates or unless cultivars are used that are hybrids of vinifera and more cold-tolerant American vines.

In order to successfully grow and market these cold-hardy grapes and their wines, and their blends with vinifera wines, Colorado growers and winemakers need to draw on the traits of self-reliance and rebellion that has served them well to this point. In this way they can not only use their Western social milieu to create wonderful new wines of distinct Colorado terroir, but also be part of the history, education and social tradition of creating new and distinctive wine legends. The status quo causes rebellion and innovation resolves it. In vino veritas.

How to store and serve wine

Brenda Wray, co-owner and wine director of 626 on Rood

By BRENDA WRAY
Co-owner and wine director of 626 on Rood
Modern American Cuisine and Wine Bar

With bare feet and the unusually hot spring weather, I sit to ponder the proper storing of wine. Where is my wine hiding to keep itself healthy, vibrant and safe from heat stroke, from cork dryness, from oxidations?

The basics are easy. Keep your wine away from sunlight, from heat, from oxygen. Don't buy your favorite wine at the store and let it sit in your car in 120-degree weather while you shop for your favorite outfit, have lunch or crack a round of golf. Keep a cooler in your car or one of those thermo bags, and keep it away from direct sun.

At home, don't leave your wine out on the counter, especially near the dishwasher or the stove, toaster or any type of compressor that will kill the fruit in the precious bottle of juice. So don't store your wine in the laundry room! Is this making sense? Heat kills wine.

There is a lot of debate about those little pumping mechanisms that take the air out of the bottle after you have a glass or two. I like to use them just to suck out that tiny bit of air, if only to give the wine a chance to be there for you the next day. No, not two weeks, just a day or so. Also, put the red wine as well as the white in the refrigerator to help keep the wine stable. Just pull the red out a half-hour before enjoying.

In Colorado, we have so many natural elements for which to be grateful. We have mountains and desert, lots of sun and snow. We don't have that Eastern humidity that

103

makes you want to droop like an overcooked pasta noodle.

Humidity, however, is a friend to a wine bottle that you want to keep for a period of time. If you have purchased a wine cooler unit, it may be practical to put a dish of water in the bottom of it. I do this and replace the water once a month. I can't be sure it works, but it makes me feel more at ease about the safety of the cork in the bottle.

Temperature is another factor in the storage and even enjoyment of wine. Whites should be served at 48°–50° F, Reds 50°–58° F. Chardonnay should be served at a higher temp than Sauvignon Blanc, and Cabernet Sauvignon at a higher temp than Pinot Noir.

Why? Chardonnay, or white Burgundy, is meant to be at a temperature that doesn't mask the fruit characters, and Pinot Noir, or Red Burgundy, is meant to be enjoyed at a cooler temperature to let the fruit dance in your glass and then in your mouth.

For those who purchase wine when traveling or have it shipped to you, let the wine rest when you get it home. Give it a couple of days to relax from the trip. This is especially true for Pinot Noir, which is a very delicate grape.

If there is an easy way to remember how

to store wine, it is this. Wine is a living, breathing organism. Treat it with respect and it will delight you back.

■

Brenda Wray and husband Chef Theo are passionate about hospitality, food and wine. Brenda's love of wine comes from the history, terroir and determination of people who put their love into a bottle.

Hermosa Vineyards tasting room on East Orchard Mesa

Colorado Mountain Winefest

By AMY NUERNBERG
Past executive director of
Colorado Mountain Winefest

After the euphoric Western Colorado oil shale boom went bust in 1982, the Grand Junction area spent a decade in an economic depression. Thousands of jobs and people left the area, and unsellable properties declined into foreclosure.

Depressed real estate prices turned out to be a good thing for start-up wineries in Palisade. By the mid-1980s, both Plum Creek Cellars and Grande River Vineyards were acquiring properties for vineyards and wineries. Colorado Mountain Vineyards and Carlson Vineyards already were open for business. A trade organization formed, named Rocky Mountain Vintners and Viticulturists.

Slowly, things started looking up in Grand Junction, and voters in 1990 passed a lodging tax to fund a Visitor & Convention Bureau. Director Debbie Kovalik came from the Colorado Springs tourism bureau, where she experienced the allure of wine while working on winemaker dinners at high-end hotels and events at Pikes Peak Vineyards.

"I knew there was a market for wine, the potential of it, based on what was happening in Colorado Springs," Debbie recalls. "There were few events here then, and Grand Junction needed something with panache to lure people from the Front Range."

Not only did she have a vision when she met with the Palisade wine group, she also had the means. Creating the first-ever Colorado wine festival was an enormous undertaking, and paying for it seemed impossible. However, the Visitor & Convention Bureau made a three-year commitment of $10,000 annually for the festival. That pledge was matched by the Colorado Wine Industry Development Board, a statewide board created in 1990 and chaired by Doug Phillips, co-owner of Plum

The harvest crush — or grape stomp — is a Winefest favorite

105

Creek.

Intended as an authentic harvest/crush festival, the Colorado Mountain Winefest debuted on a glorious fall weekend late in September of 1992. By then there were five wineries in Palisade: Carlson Vineyards, Colorado Cellars Ltd., Grande River Vineyards Winery, Plum Creek Cellars and Vail Valley Vintners. Pikes Peak Vineyards also participated.

Friday featured a Cooking with Wine seminar and lunch with a famous French chef, an Introduction to the Wine Industry talk and a Grand Tasting in the evening. Saturday, wineries poured samples for guests who paid $7 to get into the roped-off Palisade town park. A Pops concert of Gershwin tunes by the Grand Junction Symphony finished the day. Attendees were invited to take a free, self-guided tour of the wineries on Sunday.

"The festival was the stage they needed to start growing the wine business locally," Debbie says. "The VCB wanted to promote Colorado wine country tours, but the wineries needed to get to the point where they had regular tasting room hours."

Who knows how many people sipped and swayed to music that first year? Clearly the festival's plan worked: a combination of wine education, tasting and sales, with some entertainment mixed in. The template is still used, except now the festival always occupies the third weekend of September.

Over time, the number of Colorado wineries topped 100. Winefest outgrew the town park, moved to Riverbend Park and expanded to four days. In 2003 there were more than 6,000 guests — mostly from the Front Range or neighboring states.

In 2005 Colorado State University examined the economic impact of the statewide wine industry. It took a special look at the Colorado Mountain Winefest and reported it generated $2.5 million for the local economy, counting dollars spent on items such as lodging, meals, tanks of gas, bags of ice, boxes of Enstrom candy, souvenirs and bottles of wine.

Eventually Winefest went from being a fund-loser to a fundraiser for Rocky Mountain Vintners and Viticulturists, which changed its name to Colorado Association for Viticulture and Enology in 2010. The trade organization's purpose continues to be supporting grape-growing and winemaking in Colorado. Proceeds from Winefest have purchased equipment, hosted educational programs and hired experts to further the success of Colorado wines.

Colorado Mountain Winefest by the numbers

5,500 wineglasses
6,000 wine bottle tote bags
1,000 commemorative posters
1,000 T-shirts
350 Riedel VIP glasses
300 volunteers
50 wineries

Brent Helleckson of Stone Cottage Cellars pours at Colorado Mountain Winefest

By AMY NUERNBERG
Past executive director of Colorado Mountain Winefest

Utilizing their friendships with top-notch Colorado artists, avid art collectors and Plum Creek Winery owners Doug and Sue Phillips had a goal when they recruited artwork for early Colorado Mountain Winefest posters.

"We wanted the poster to be collectible and to elevate the perception of Winefest as a fun, upscale wine festival," recalls Sue. "It worked." Elements of art prints were incorporated, such as titles, artist name, medium and the artist signing a limited number of prints.

They invited Gerald Fritzler, American Watercolor Society member, to paint "plein air" (outdoors) at the intimate, tree-canopied Palisade Town Park in 1999. His loose and vivid watercolor became the popular 2000 commemorative poster.

For the 10th anniversary poster, the Phillipses commissioned longtime friend

1992 Wilda Fortune, watercolor (1st annual)

1993 Herb Sanders, photography; Christopher Tomlinson, concept (2nd annual)

and renowned Colorado landscape watercolorist Buffalo Kaplinski to create a lively vista of rolling vineyards under a dramatic sky surrounding a blissful couple. A colorful close-up of ripe wine grapes by Kaplinski followed in 2002.

Growing pains in 1998

In the 1990s, attendance at Winefest and the market for posters were slowly growing, while poster storage space was rapidly shrinking. "We were sitting on so many leftover posters, in 1998 we decided

1994 Amy Nuernberg, graphic illustration; "Wine is One of the Finer Things in Life" (3rd annual)

1995 Karl Nicholason, acrylics (4th annual)

1996 Kitty Nicholason, graphic illustration (5th annual)

1997 Diana Woods, oil; "Palisade Vineyard" (6th & 7th annual)

to skip buying art and reuse the 1997 Mount Garfield image again on the festival brochure," says John Lowey, first executive director of the Colorado Wine Industry Development Board and a volunteer Winefest organizer. "Soon after, Winefest changed dramatically and went from around 1,300 to 4,000 festival-goers, and the Gerald Fritzler and Buffalo Kaplinski posters were very popular."

Public votes on artwork

Inspired by the art show at the Meeker Sheepdog Trials, a Winefest fan and artist advocated for a similar competition to select art for the annual Winefest poster. "First getting a good assortment of art to choose from, then displaying and hopefully selling all the entries in an art exhibit made it a success for both the event and the artists," says artist/teacher Kimmer High-Jepson.

The first art competition drew many entries. Palisade's Blue Pig Gallery hosted the show, and the winner was the grape-stomping chefs of 2007. Giving the public a chance to vote was introduced the next year. Since 2008 a Winefest committee narrows the entries to three poster contenders, and on opening night at the Blue Pig attendees sip Colorado wine and vote for their favorite to become the next commemorative poster. By the way, Kimmer's artwork won with her take on a bucking bronc theme in 2008.

Own your own Winefest art

The Colorado Mountain Winefest is the principal fundraiser for CAVE, which is an acronym for the trade group Colorado Association of Vintners and Enologists. With some 60 members, CAVE, based in Palisade, Colo., supports winemaking and viticulture throughout the state.

Current and past Winefest posters and T-shirts are available for sale at Winefest every year; at the CAVE office, 144 Kluge Ave., Palisade; and at www.winecolorado.org.

Most posters are $15.

CAVE purchases the original artwork for Winefest posters and someday may do

1999 Molly Davis Gough, watercolor (8th annual)

2000 Gerald J. Fritzler, A.W.S., watercolor; "Afternoon at the Winefest" (9th annual)

2001 Buffalo Kaplinski, watercolor; "Taste the Harvest" (10th anniversary)

2002 Buffalo Kaplinski, watercolor; "Treasure of Sangiovese" (11th annual)

more with their growing fine-art collection. Meanwhile they just enjoy it on their office walls.

Wine not only libation, but medium

Wine paint? Really?

And what does a cruise ship, an American Pop-art artist and a Dutch Golden Age painter have to do with a Winefest poster?

When artists Gary Hauschulz and wife Susan Metzger retired from teaching art, they booked a celebratory three-week ocean cruise. Gary wanted to paint portraits, and to simplify luggage, he decided to paint with his drinks: coffee in the morning and wine in the evening.

Once aboard, "I remembered an image from Franz Halz of delightful people, they were so doggone happy and holding mugs and flutes," Gary says of the 17th century Dutch painter. "I looked for happy faces."

But when he started working with wine, "I was hugely disappointed — even the darkest wine was a blush," he says. "So I started leaving a few sips in the wine glass and taking it back to our cabin where it could dry out and concentrate."

Back home in Palisade, he went around to the wineries for his art supplies. He eventually used concentrated pigments from 12 different wines, including fruit wines.

How about the Pop-art painter? "The pop artist, Larry Rivers, has a painting where he labeled the parts of the face," Gary cites as its influence on his 2012 "Red, Wine & Fruit" artwork. "I really like the idea of the wineries having their wines labeled on the poster."

2003 Mary Moss watercolor; "Vendemmia" (Italian for Post-Harvest Party) (12th annual)

2004 Laura Bradford, Amy Nuernberg, graphic illustration; "Vintage Colorado Winefest Trail" (13th annual)

2005 Len Chmiel, oil; "Vineyard Mosaic" (14th annual)

2006 Sara Alyn Oakley, oil; "Colorado Uncorked" (15th anniversary)

2007 Carole Katchen, pastel; "Kick Up Your Heels" (16th annual)

2008 Kimmer High-Jepson, pastel; "And you thought our wines were TAME?" (17th annual)

2009 Mary Ellen Andrews, acrylics;
"Labor of Love" (18th annual)

2011 Patricia Carroll, acrylics; "Colorado Nectar"
(20th anniversary)

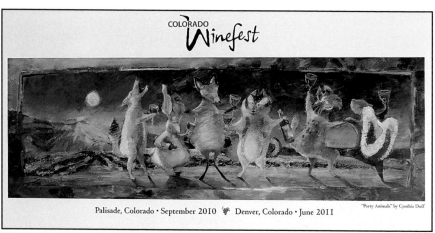

2010 Cynthia Duff, acrylics; "Party Animals" (19th annual)

2012 Gary Hauschulz, Colorado wine pigment; "Red, White & Fruit" (21st annual)

2013 Judy Rogan, acrylics and multi-media; "Tipsy Trails" (22nd annual)

Acknowledgments

Admittedly, a book of this sort at first didn't sound much like heavy lifting. However, under the polish of promise was the core of uncovering and conveying what it is that drives otherwise sensible people to couple their lives to an enterprise where much is out of their control.

It goes without pause that this project was not done in a vacuum and that whatever virtues appear within the following people should share the credit. Without their support and contributions, this story still would be hanging on the vine, so to speak.

The entire endeavor would not have happened without the support of *Daily Sentinel* publisher Jay Seaton, so if readers enjoy this book, thank him.

The heartbeat of this book is Laurena Davis of *The Daily Sentinel*, well-spring of much behind-the-scenes writing, editing and guidance. Laurena merited utmost respect and gratitude for sensitively navigating the project with skill, vision and equanimity, masterly qualities of utmost importance whether riding herd on this enterprise or offering direction to her trio of children.

Sincere thanks and profound appreciation go to *Daily Sentinel* graphics artist Robert García, who repeatedly demonstrated his considerable talent with the computer arts while displaying the pragmatic ability of keeping us focused on the matters at hand.

Grand Junction designer Amy Nuernberg is a longtime friend and colleague and her inclusion to the project proved invaluable on a regular basis. Her thoughtful suggestions and insights to the state's wine industry enriched the experience.

Thanks, too, to the talented staff photographers of *The Daily Sentinel* — Gretel Daugherty, Dean Humphrey and Christopher Tomlinson.

Priscilla Mangnall, assistant to the publisher, cheerfully managed the not-easy task of chasing down information from recalcitrant winemakers, a chore not unlike being nibbled to death by a duck.

There also were the generous and wine-smart columnists whose only mistakes were answering the phone when we called. Appreciation goes to state enologist Stephen Menke, state viticulturist Horst Caspari, restaurateur and wine savant Brenda Wray, winemaker Lee Bradley and the owner-winemaker team from Plum Creek Winery, Sue Phillips and Jenne Baldwin-Eaton. If I've left out others, it is my error of listing and not any shortage of gratitude for their contributions.

Additionally, appreciation goes to Cassidee Shull and Sandie Cooper at the Colorado Association for Viticulture and Enology and Doug Caskey, executive director for the Colorado Wine Industry Development Board.

And of course, this book never would have been written without the support, encouragement and friendship of many Colorado winemakers, all of whom offered insight and advice while patiently tolerating a nosy writer with the curiosity of a 5-year-old.

Among them: Guy Drew, John Sutcliffe, Brent and Karen Helleckson, Joan and John Mathewson, Lee and Kathy Bradley, Anna and Lance Hanson, Bob Witham (who taught me more about the wine business than I can acknowledge), Stephen and Naomi Smith, Bennett and Davy Price, Sue Phillips, Glenn Foster, Parker Carlson, Scott and Theresa High, Diana Read, Dr. Gerald Ivancie and Liz Kennedy Ivancie, the staff at the Museum of Western Colorado and countless others whose names may not appear but whose contributions have not been forgotten.

A special note of gratitude goes to Jenne Baldwin-Eaton of Plum Creek Winery and Nancy Janes and John Behr of Whitewater Hill Vineyards, who repeatedly have demonstrated saintly forbearance and remarkable tolerance.

And a special thanks to you, the readers who express an interest in and curiosity for Colorado wines.

Photo credits

Azura Cellars: 52
Buchanan, Dave: 41, 48, 61, 72, 97
Canyon Wind Cellars: 10, 11
COLTERRIS: 15
Cottonwood Cellars: 43
Cox, Jim: 87
Delta Tourism Board: 1
Frost, Doug/courtesy of: VII
Grand Junction Visitor & Convention Bureau: II, X, 3, 8
Daugherty, Gretel: IX, XI, 16, 76, 77, 91, 95, 101, 103
Guy Drew Vineyards: 4, 80, 81
Humphrey, Dean: I, VI, 2, 39, 49, 59, 62, 92, 94, 96
Ivancie Family Collection: 88
Jack Rabbit Hill Winery: 58
Museum of Western Colorado: 87
Museum of Western Colorado /The Daily Sentinel Collection/Al Gibes: 90
Museum of Western Colorado /The Daily Sentinel Collection/Bob Grant: 89
Museum of Western Colorado /The Daily Sentinel Collection/Jill Kaplan: 90
Nuernberg, Amy : 51, 89
Stine, Penny: 7, 102
Stone Cottage Cellars: 67, 68
Sutcliffe Vineyards: 84, 85
Tomlinson, Christopher : XII, 5, 29, 30, 34, 35, 65, 71, 75, 99, 100, 104, 105, 106, cover flap, inside back cover

INDEX

Note: Numbers in *italic* refer to photographs. Numbers in **bold** refer to maps.

1winedude.com, 81
47-Ten Wines, 11
626 on Rood, *103*
5680' Vineyards, 53

A

agricultural history of Palisade, 87–90
Alfred Eames Cellars, 54
Alsace (France), 71–72
American Viticultural Area (AVA)
Grand Valley, 8, 17, 24, 89
West Elks, 52, 53, 54, 63, 64
An American Provence (Huber), 51, 61
Ancestral Puebloans, 77, 80, 81, 84
Andrews, Mary Ellen, 112
Anemoi Wines, 10–11
annual horticultural process, 99–100
apple cider makers, 57, 65
Appleseed, Johnny, 65
Argentina vineyards, 16, 71
Ariza, Max, 85
Aroma Wheel, Wine, 93
artwork
for Colorado Mountain Winefest, 107–13
at wineries, 18, 29–31, 46, 55, 66, 74
Aspen Times, 82
Avant Vineyards, 9
Azura Cellars, *52*, 55

B

Baldwin-Eaton, Jenne, 31, *91*
Barbier, John, 26
Behrs, John, 38
Big B's Fabulous Juices, 65, 66
biodynamic winery, 58–60
Black Bridge Winery, 56, 99–100
Bleak, Allan and Elizabeth, 83
blind tasting, VII
blogs about wine, 10, 81
Blossomwood Cidery, 57
Blue Pig Gallery, 108
Bordeaux (France), VIII
Boulder Creek Winery, 8
Bradford, Laura, 110
Bradley, Kathy, 56
Bradley, Lee, 56, 99–100
Bruner, Erik, 29, 30, 44
Buckel, Joe, 85, 86

Burgundy (France), VIII

C

California vineyards, VII, VIII, XI, 1, 11, 12, 88
Canyons of the Ancients National Monument, *76*
Canyon Wind Cellars, 7, 10–12, *95*
Carlson, Mary, 2, 13, *90*
Carlson, Parker, 2–3, 13, *90, 92*
Carlson Vineyards, 2–3, 8, 13, *90, 92*, 105
Carney, Janese and Shawn, 57
Carr, Jeff and Carol, 20
Carroll, Patricia, 112
Caspari, Horst, 3, *97*
Catena, Nicola, 16
CAVE. *see* Colorado Association for Viticulture and Enology (CAVE)
Chapman, John, 65
Chicago Field Museum, 13
Child, Julia, 88
Chmiel, Len, 111
Christianson, Ellen, 12
Christianson, Jay, 7, 10–12, *95*
Christianson, Jennifer, 7, 10–12
Christianson, Norman, 7, 10, 12
cider makers, 57, 65
Classic Wines, 16
climate and conditions
of Argentina vineyards, 16
of Burgundy vineyards, VIII
of Western Colorado vineyards, VII–VIII, 2, 9, 16, 17
Colorado Association for Viticulture and Enology (CAVE), 29–30, 105, 106, 109–10
Colorado Cellars, 14, 89
Colorado Mountain Vineyards, 2, 14, 21, *89, 90*, 105
Colorado Mountain Winefest
about, 8, 105–6
posters for, 107–13
Colorado State University
2005 study of wine industry, 106
Four Corners Project, 14, 52, 72, 89, 97–98
Research Station, 68
Colorado wine industry
future of, 4, 90

history of, XI, 7–8, 16, 29, 102, 105
pioneer of, 18, 29
varietals of, 98
Colorado Wine Industry Development
Act, 8, 30
Board, 105
COLTERRIS Wines, 15–17
Coors Brewing Company, 2
Cortez Journal, 82
Cottonwood Cellars, 43–45
Coyote Creek Art Gallery, 18
Crawford, George A., 8, 87, 97
Cussler, Clive, 31

D

Daily Sentinel, The (Grand Junction), 82
Davis, Wink, 64
DeBeque Canyon Winery, 18, 90
Delicious Orchards, 65
Demeter Biodynamic certified, 60
Denver Post, 31, 82
Desert Sun Vineyards & Winery, *XII*, 19
Doyle, Kevin, 74
Drew, Guy, *4*, 80–82
Drew, Ruth, 80, 82
dry farming vineyards, 26, 81
Duff, Cynthia, 112
Dunn, Kenn, 24, 98
Durango Herald, The, 82
Durango tasting rooms, 78, 85

E

Edible Aspen, 60
education in winemaking, 10, 21, 68, 71, 85,
93
Eisele, Max, 64
Elk Mountains, *51, 72. see also* West Elks
American Viticultural Area
Engineering School of Enology, 71
Enstrom Candies, 13, 106
experimental growing in Western Colorado,
98. *see also* Colorado State University;
hybrid winemaking

F

Facebook, 10
Fagner, Dean and Tracy, 78
first commercial vineyard
in Colorado, XI, 14, 88, 97
in Grand Valley, 8
to use only Colorado-grown grapes, 14, 29
Fitzgerald, F. Scott, 10

Flowers Winery, 85
Fortune, Wilda, 107
Foster, Glenn and Natalie, 27, 33
Four Corners
about, 77
wineries map, **76**
Four Corners Project, Colorado State
University, 14, 52, 72, 89, 97–98
Four Corners Regional Commission, 89,
97–98
Four Leaves Winery, 78
Foxfire books, 79
Fox Fire Farms Winery & Vineyards, 79
France vineyards
Alsace, 71
Bordeaux, VIII
Burgundy, VIII
comparison to, VII, 52, 61, 64
Loire Valley of, 26
Provence, 51, 61–62
Fresh & Wyld Farmhouse Inn, 53
Fritzler, Gerald J., 107, 109
Frost, Doug, *VII*, VIII, 11
Fruit Belt of Mesa County, The (pamphlet,
1896), 7
Fruitlands Forever initiative, 90
fruit production, various, 47, 99–100
future of Colorado wine, 4, 90, 102

G

Gannett, Henry, 42
gardens, 17, 37
Garfield Estates Vineyard & Winery, 20
Garrett, Dave and Pamela, 46
Garrett Estate Cellars, 46
Gazette, The (Colorado Springs), 82
geologic history of Western Colorado, IX
Gillespie, Helen and Ty, 55
Goebel, Lynn and Vaughn, 32
Gough, Molly Davis, 109
Grande River Vineyards, *X*, 21, 90, 105
Grand Junction history, 105. *see also* Grand
Valley
Grand Junction Symphony, 106
Grand River Ditch Company, 7
Grand Valley, *5. see also* Palisade history
American Viticultural Area, 8, 17, 24, 89
wine industry of, 7–8, 87–90, 97, 105
wineries map, **6**
Grand Valley Irrigation Company, 7
grapes, *48, 68*
harvesting, 8, 99–100

Graystone Winery, 22
Gros, Yvon, 3, 4, 61–63
Guard, Neil and Diane, 9
Gubbini, Linda Lee, 23
Gubbini Winery, 23
Guy Drew Vineyards, *4*, 80–82

H

Halz, Franz, 110
Hamman Jr., Richard A., 98
Hanson, Anna, 58, 60
Hanson, Lance, 58–60
harvesting grapes, *8*, 99–100
harvest party gatherings, 83, 86
Harvests of Joy (Mondavi), 15
Hauschulz, Gary, 110, 113
heat and storing wine, 103–4
Helleckson, Brent, 3, 67–69
Helleckson, Karen, 67–69
Hermosa Vineyards, 24, 98, *104*
High, Matthew, 16
High, Scott, 15–16
High, Theresa, 15–17
high-altitude vineyards, VIII, 2, 17, 64,
    71–73, 83, 98
High Country Orchards & Vineyards, 15–17
highest winery, 3, 71–73
High-Jepson, Kimmer, 108, 111
honey wine makers, 27
Horse Mountain, *II*
Horse Mountain Vineyards, 23
horticultural annual processes, 99–100
Hovde, Doug and Kathryn, 19
Huber, Thomas P., 51, 61, 62
humidity and storing wine, 103–4
hybrid winemaking, 4, 35, 77, 81, 98, 102

I

icewine makers, 38
immigrant viticulturists in Grand Valley,
    7–8, 87, 97
industry, wine. *see* Colorado wine industry;
    Western Colorado
Infinite Monkey Theorem Winery, 85
Italy vineyards, 15
Ivancie, Gerald, XI, 88–89, 97
Ivancie, Mary, *88*, 89
Ivancie Cellars, 88–89

J

Jack Rabbit Hill Winery, *VI*, 58–60
James Beard Award, 59, 60

Janes, Nancy, 38
Johnson and Wales University, 85
Jones, Alberta and Evelyn, 79
Jones, Arthur and Dovie, 79
Judgement of Paris (1976), VII

K

Kahil Winery, 25
Kaplinski, Buffalo, 107, 109
Katchen, Carole, 111
keeving technique, 57
Kimball, Rob, 53
Kovalik, Debbie, 105

L

language of wine, 93–96
Larson, Shawn, 65, 66
lavender
gardens, 17, 37
wine, 33
Lawson, Kathryn, 25
Lawson, Tyrel, 17, 25, 35
Leroux Creek Inn and Vineyards, 3, 61–63
Lowey, John, 108

M

Maison la Belle Vie, 26
Make Your Own Wine service, 78
maps
Four Corners, **76**
Grand Valley, **6**
North Fork Valley, **50**
Uncompahgre Valley, **40**
Mathewson, Joan, 3–4, 51, 71–73
Mathewson, John, 51, 71–73
Maurer, Barbara and Robert, 22
McElmo Canyon, 77, 80–82, 84–86
Meadery of the Rockies, 27
Menke, Stephen, VIII, 4, *101*
mentoring within wine community, 2–3, 11,
    29–30
Mesa Land Trust, 90
Mesa Park Vineyards, 28
Mesa Verde National Park, 75
Mesa Winds Winery, 64
methode champenoise, 14
Metzger, Susan, 110
"Million Dollar Breeze," 7, 11
Mondavi, Robert, 15
Moss, Mary, 110
Mountain View Winery, 47

Mount Garfield, 5, 9, 10, 108
music concerts, 21, 106

N

Napa (California) vineyards, VII, VIII, XI, 11, 12, 88
Neal, Bret, 70
next generation winemakers, 10–12
Nicholason, Karl, 108
Nicholason, Kitty, 108
Nichols, Lyle, 31
Noble, Ann C., 93
North Fork Cellars, 65–66
North Fork Valley, *1, 49*
about, 51–52
wineries map, **50**
Nuernberg, Amy, *87,* 105, 107, 110

O

Oakley, Sara Alyn, 111
Obama, Michelle, 15
Olathe Winery, The, 43–45
Orchard Mesa Research Station, 97–98. *see also* Colorado State University
Orchard Valley Farms & Market, 56
organic wineries, certified, 58–60, 62, 64, 79, 86
Origin of Certain Place Names in the United States, The (Gannett), 42

P

painting with wine, 110, 113
Palisade Fruit and Wine Byway, *7,* 8, 16
Palisade history, 87–90, 105–6. *see also* Grand Valley
Palma Cigar Store, 74
Parry, Evan and Alberta (Jones), 79
Parry, Linda and Richard, 79
Parsons, Ben, 85
Payne, Glenn and Evelyn (Jones), 79
peach industry, 9, 15, 34, 89, 100
Peak Spirits Distillery, 58, 59
pear cider makers, 57
Pepi, Robert, 11, 12
Petersen, Alfred Eames, 54
Phillips, Doug, 29–30, 105, 107
Phillips, Sue, 29–31, *91,* 107
Pikes Peak Vineyards, 2, 105
Playboy, 81
Pleasant View Vineyards, 83
Plum Creek Winery (aka Plum Creek Cellars), 2, 29–31, 44, 90, 96, 105

posters for Colorado Mountain Winefest, 107–13
pottery shards, ancient, *77*
Price, Bennett and Davelyn, 18, 90
Price, Chuck and Patty, 28
production
of Colorado wineries, 8
of different varietals, 98
prohibition, 8, 65, 87–88, 97
pronounciation guide, wine, 94
Provence (France), 51, 61–62
Ptarmigan Vineyards, 70

R

Read, Diana and Keith, 43–45
Reckert, Joanna, 61–63
regional expression, 20
Rivers, Larry, 110
Roagan, Judy, 113
Roberts, Joe, 81
Rocky Mountain Vineyards, 14
Rocky Mountain Vintners and Viticulturists, 105, 106. *see also* Colorado Association for Viticulture and Enology (CAVE)
rose gardens, 17, 37
Rothschild, Baron Phillipe, 15

S

Sanders, Herb, 107
San Juan Mountains, *39, 40*
Schwartz, Jeff and Tracey, 65
Schwartz, Seth, 65
second-generation winemakers, 7, 10–12
Seewald, Ann, 2, 89
Seewald, Jim, 2, 21, 89
Shock Wave (Cussler), 31
Sinskey, Robert, 11
Smith, Naomi, 21
Smith, Stephen, 21, 90
social history of wine, 101–2
social media, 10, 81
Stag's Leap Winery, 88
state enologist. *see* Menke, Steve
state viticulturist. *see* Caspari, Horst
Steinman, Harvey, 74
Stevens, Brian, 27, 33
St. Kathryn Cellars, 27, 33
Stone Cottage Cellars, 3, 67–69
Stoney Mesa Winery, 70
storing wine, 103–4
Summit Cellars, 32

sunlight and storing wine, 103
Sunset, 81
Sutcliffe, John, 84–86
Sutcliffe Vineyards, 84–86

T

Talon Winery, 27, 33
tasting, wine, VII, XI, 91–93
Tavern on the Green restaurant, 84
tax
lodging, 105
wine, 90
temperature and storing wine, 104
terroir, understanding, VII, 4, 62
Terror Creek Winery, 3, *51*, 71–73
Thoma, Rainer, 20, 21
Thonon-les-Bains Cooking School, 62, 63
Time article, "The United States of Wine," 31
Tomlinson, Christopher, 107
tourism, wine, 8, 16, 105. see also Colorado
     Mountain Winefest
Trip Advisor, 8
Turley, Padte and Richard, 14
Tuscany (Italy), 15
Twitter, 10
Two Rivers Winery & Chateau, 17, 25,
     34–36, 92

U

Uncompahgre Valley
about, 41–42
wineries map, **40**
"The United States of Wine," *Time* article, 31
University of California, Davis, 68, 93
University of Denver, 21

V

Valley Fruit and Wine Shop, 18
Varaison Vineyards & Winery, 37
varietals grown in Colorado, 98
Vaynerchuk, Gary, 81
Vineland Corporation, The, 14
Visitor & Convention Bureau (Grand
     Junction), 105
Vitis lambrusca, 87
Vitis vinifera, 77, 87, 98, 102
vocabulary, wine, 95–96

W

Wade, Sam, 42
Washington Post, The, 81

Washington State University, 23
Webb, Brad and Brooke, 28
wedding tradition, 27
West, Kristin and Ron, 37
West Elks American Viticultural Area, 52,
     53, 54, 63, 64. *see also* Elk Mountains
Western Colorado. *see also* Grand Valley
climate and conditions of, VIII, 14, 16, 17,
     18, 35, 98
geologic history of, IX
wine industry of, I, 7–8, 16, 87–90, 97, 105
Westword, 82
Whitewater Hill Vineyards, 38
wine
appreciation, XI
Colorado varietals, 98
history of, 101
language of, 93–96
painting with, 110, 113
social history of, 101–2
storing, 103–4
tasting, VII, XI, 91–93
tourism, 8, 16, 105
Wine Aroma Wheel, 93
Wine Enthusiast Magazine, 85
The Wine Industry Development Act of
     1990, 90
"Wine Library" television show, 81
Wine Spectator scoring, 69, 74, 85
Winiarski, Warren, 88–89
Witham, Billie, 34–36
Witham, Bob, 34–36
Woods, Diana, 108
Woody Creek Cellars, 74
Wray, Brenda, 103–4
Wright, Gary, 26

Y

Young, Mike and Wendy, 47

NOTES

NOTES